EMUs: A HISTORY

Hugh Llewelyn

AMBERLEY

First published 2016

Amberley Publishing
The Hill, Stroud
Gloucestershire, GL5 4EP

www.amberley-books.com

Copyright © Hugh Llewelyn, 2016

The right of Hugh Llewelyn to be identified as the Author of this work has been asserted in accordance with the Copyrights, Designs and Patents Act 1988.

ISBN 978 1 4456 4982 5 (print)
ISBN 978 1 4456 4983 2 (ebook)

British Library Cataloguing in Publication Data.
A catalogue record for this book is available from the British Library.

Typeset in 10pt on 12pt Sabon LT Std.
Typesetting by Amberley Publishing.
Printed in the UK.

Contents

Introduction   5

1   First Generation EMUs – Standard BR Mark 1 Designs 1953–74 and BR-built Pre-nationalisation Designs of
    the LMS (1938)–1958; LNER 1949–50 and SR (1938)–1958   7

2   First Generation EMUs – Standard BR Mark 2 Designs 1965–77   44

3   Early Second Generation EMUs – BR 1972 Designs 1971–81   46

4   Later Second Generation EMUs – Standard BR Mark 3 Designs 1981–95   58

5   Third Generation EMUs – Designs Towards and under Privatisation: BREL/ABB Networker Family 1991–95   86

6   Third Generation EMUs – Designs Towards and under Privatisation: Hunslet Transportation Projects 1992–93   92

7   Third Generation EMUs – Designs under Privatisation: CAF/Siemens Family 1997–98   95

8   Third Generation EMUs – Designs under Privatisation: Alstom Juniper Family 1998   98

9   Third Generation EMUs – Designs under Privatisation: Adtranz/Bombardier Electrostar Family 1999 and Continuing   104

10 Third Generation EMUs – Designs under Privatisation: Alstom Pendolino 2001–12   116

11 Third Generation EMUs – Designs under Privatisation: Siemens Desiro Family 2002 and Continuing   118

12 Third Generation EMUs – Designs under Privatisation: Hitachi Javelin 2006–11   125

Bibliography   126

Abbreviations   128

Introduction

This book aims to give a brief illustrated history of all EMUs built since the formation of British Railways in 1948. The first section includes both those classes designed by the pre-nationalisation companies but which were constructed by BR and those of BR's own designs based on their standard Mark 1 coach – the 'first generation' EMUs. Initially, it seemed sensible to separate out these two types, except that on the Southern Region there were many classes which contained both types, for example, the Class 4-EPB (or Class 415) EMUs contained sets based both on the standard BR Mark 1 coach and the Southern Railway coach designed by OVS Bulleid. It would have been logical if BR (SR) had given the two types separate classifications, but this was not the case. Therefore, I have included both types in chapter 1. The second section of the book includes the two classes of EMU based on the semi-integrally constructed standard BR Mark 2 coach body, but as they used slam doors they are usually considered members of the first generation.

The third section is of the early designs of BR's second generation EMUs, termed the '1972 design'. The fourth section is of the later designs of BR's second generation EMUs using the standard BR Mark 3 coach body of full monocoque construction. Chapters 5–11 contain the third generation EMUs built by the privatised BREL workshops or private rolling stock constructors for the sectorised BR and then the private owners of rolling stock.

Restrictions of space do not allow a comprehensive history or full technical details of each class – other books do that for the various classes, as given in the bibliography. The same restriction means that the first generation EMUs do not have an illustration of every class; some similar classes have been combined under a single entry. Also, for reasons of space and because some classes are not really a part of the mainstream history of EMUs, it has been decided to exclude the Advanced Passenger Train prototype, the former tube stock used on the Isle of Wight and on the Waterloo & City line, and Eurostar trains. The photographs are largely my own, apart from two which are credited accordingly. Within chapters 1, 2 and 3, classes are described in numerical class order except that the prototype Classes 445 and 446 are first in chapter 2 and the prototype Class 457/316 is first in chapter 3, as both gave rise to the classes that followed. As to chapters 4–11, these are arranged into 'families' of classes designed by each manufacturer so that a better appreciation of the development of each type is gained. The manufacturer groupings are in the order of their introduction and within each group by class number.

It is an exciting time for EMU enthusiasts, with new classes in the process of being constructed – Siemens' 'Desiro City' Class 700 for Thameslink and Class 707 for South West Trains, Bombardier's Class 345 'Aventra' for Crossrail, Hitachi's AT200 for ScotRail and Hitachi's AT300 (Classes 800 and 801) for the soon to be electrified Great Western main line.

First Generation EMUs – Standard BR Mark 1 Designs 1953–74 and BR-built Pre-nationalisation Designs of the LMS (1938)–1958; LNER: 1949–50 and SR (1938)–1958

BR (York and Doncaster) Standard Mark 1 25 kV AC/6.25 kV AC Overhead Outer Suburban Class 302 (Class AM2) Four-car EMUs

On nationalisation in 1948, British Railways produced standard coach designs for express and suburban services in both loco-hauled and multiple-unit forms, designated BR Mark 1. The Class AM2 EMUs (later reclassified under TOPS as Class 302, then 302/2) were of the outer suburban variety of this standard design, with rather unimaginatively 'styled' slab cab fronts.

BR's Doncaster and York works built 112 sets in 1959–60 for the Eastern Region's overhead 25 kV AC (with inner London sections originally 6.25 kV AC until upgraded) electrified London, Tilbury and Southend line from Fenchurch Steet to Shoeburyness. Since they worked long outer suburban services, they were gangwayed within sets (though only after refurbishment) and had both first- and second-class accommodation. They were essentially a four-car version of the Class AM7s (later Class 307). Seven sets were converted to three-car units in 1989–90 – four sets for parcels use as Class 302/9 and three for departmental use as Class 937. All were withdrawn from service by 1999.

Pressed Steel Class 303 (Class AM3) and Cravens Class 311 (Class AM11) Standard BR Mark 1 25 kV AC/6.25 kV AC Overhead Inner Suburban Glasgow Blue Train Three-car EMUs

In 1959–61, Pressed Steel's Linwood factory built ninety-one three-car Class AM11 (Class 311 under TOPS) EMUs for the ScR's North Clyde and Cathcart Circle suburban lines, newly electrified on the 25 kV AC overhead system in 1960, although some sections of the line operated with just 6.25 kV AC. The cars were based on the BR Mark 1 bodyshell but extensively redesigned to have sliding doors – the first EMU designed by BR to have this feature (previous EMUs with sliding doors had been designed by the LNER or LMS). The more streamlined cabs with wraparound windows was another feature which made these units seem so much more modern than previous EMUs with slam doors and slab fronts. They had all second-class accommodation and no gangways.

On their introduction, the Class 303s experienced considerable trouble with blown transformers, which resulted in the temporary reintroduction of steam services until the faults could be rectified. They were later used on the Inverclyde and Argyle lines following

BR (ER) Class 302 (or Class AM2) outer suburban four-car EMU, No. 238 (later No. 302 238) in rail blue at Upminster, March 1976.

Pictured at Upminster on a Fenchurch Street–Southend–Shoeburyness service is Class 302 (or Class AM2) four-car EMU No. 232 (later No. 302 232) in rail blue, March 1976.

Surmounting Bethnal Green Bank on a Liverpool Street–Southbury–Bishops Stortford service is Class 302 (or Class AM2) four-car EMU No. 210 (later No. 302 210) in rail blue and grey livery, September 1982.

Strathclyde PTE Class 303 inner suburban three-car EMU No. 303 006 (no longer a Blue Train!) at Glasgow Central, 1 March 2001. (Photograph courtesy Gordon Edgar)

their electrification. In the early 1980s several sets were transferred to work in the Liverpool/Crewe/Manchester areas, displacing Class 506s amongst other older classes. The north-west sets were withdrawn in the 1990s but those still working in Glasgow survived until 2002.

When the Inverclyde lines were electrified in 1967, nineteen more units, very similar to the Class 303s but with updated details, were built by Cravens of Sheffield and classed AM11 (later TOPS Class 311). Over time they were used interchangeably with the Class 303s. Curiously, although the Class 303s were refurbished, the Class 311s were not and were withdrawn in the 1990s, the Class 303s outliving them. The last two surviving Class 311s were in departmental use (as Class 936) and lasted until 1999.

BR (Wolverton) Standard Mark 1 25 kV AC/6.25kV AC Overhead Outer Suburban Class 304 (Class AM4) Three- and Four-car EMUs

The Class 304s (or AM4s) were of standard BR Mark 1 (1959) design for the LMR's overhead 25 kV AC (with some sections 6.25kV AC initially) newly electrified WCML outer suburban services and had first- and second-class accommodation. They were built as four-car units by BR, Wolverton: fifteen Class 304/1 sets in 1960 for Crewe–Manchester services and, in 1961, twenty Class 304/2s for Crewe–Liverpool services (although at first some were temporarily allocated to the ER's Liverpool Street–Southend Victoria services) and ten Class 304/3s for Crewe–Rugby services. The latter two 1961 subclasses had revised seating and equipment. Gradually usage spread to the Birmingham/Rugby/Northampton area and even to Euston.

In the early 1980s the sets were refurbished and reduced to three-car formations, without the Trailer Composite. They were not built with

gangways, even though they were designed for outer suburban services and, surprisingly, the refurbishment scheme did not include their fitting as occurred with other classes such as the AM5s (or 305). All sets were withdrawn by 1996.

BR (York and Doncaster) Standard Mark 1 25 kV AC/6.25 kV AC Overhead Inner/Outer Suburban Class 305 (Class AM5) Three- and Four-car EMUs

The Class 305 was of standard BR Mark 1 (1959) design. The fifty-five Class 305/1 three-car sets were built by BR's York works in 1960 for the ER's 25 kV AC (and 6.25 kV AC initially) Liverpool Street–Tottenham Hale–Hertford East and Liverpool Street–Enfield/Chingford lines' inner suburban services. They were non-gangwayed with all second-class accommodation. In the same year, BR's Doncaster works built nineteen Class 305/2 four-car sets for the Lea Valley Line (Liverpool Street–Southbury–Hertford East/Bishops Stortford) outer suburban services and, like other such longer-range EMUs, had first- and second-class accommodation but were not gangwayed.

In 1985–92 twenty-four Class 305/1s were refurbished and had a Trailer Composite from a Class 302 (AM2) added to form a four-car unit with two-class accommodation, being reclassified 305/2. In addition, gangways within the set were installed, which also applied to the Class 305/2s built as such when refurbished at the same time. In 1991 some Class 305/2s were reduced to three-car sets and facelifted (losing their first class accommodation) when transferred to the north-west (Greater Manchester PTE), a few later regaining their fourth car. Five four-car Class 305/2s were yet again moved to Edinburgh to work North Berwick services. In 1984 one three-car set was converted for departmental use as a Class 305/9. All were withdrawn by 2001.

BR (LMR) Class 304/3 (or Class AM4/3) outer suburban four-car EMU No. 041 (later No. 304 041) in rail blue nears Crewe on a Manchester Piccadilly–Altrincham service, May 1975.

Class 304/1 (or Class AM4/1) four-car outer suburban EMU No. 304 043 (ex-No. 043) of BR Regional Railways/Greater Manchester PTE but still in rail blue and grey livery at Manchester Piccadilly on a Wilmslow service, October 1992.

BR (ER) Class 305/1 (or Class AM5/1) inner suburban three-car EMU No. 412 (later No. 305 412) in rail blue and grey mounting Bethnal Green Bank on a Liverpool Street–Cheshunt service, September 1982.

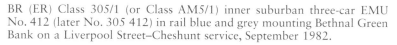

Seen at Manchester (London Road) on a service to Crewe via Stockport in October 1992 is Class 305/2 (Class AM5/2) outer suburban four-car EMU No. 305 515 (ex-No. 515) in BR Provincial Railways livery.

Metropolitan Cammell (Saltley) and Birmingham Railway Carriage & Wagon Co. (Smethwick) LNER 1,500 V DC Overhead, later 25 kV AC/6.25 kV AC Overhead Inner Suburban Class 306 (Class AM6) Three-car EMUs

These sets were ordered by the LNER from Metropolitan Cammell of Saltley and the Birmingham Railway & Carriage Co. of Smethwick before the Second World War but the ninety-two sets built did not appear until 1949 and were thus delivered to BR (Eastern Region). The class were designed for the Great Eastern services on the Liverpool Street–Shenfield line, the electrification of which had begun before the war but was not completed until 1949. The system used was the 1,500 V DC overhead one. As electrification extended to Chelmsford and Southend Victoria, in 1956 the class spread to these routes. The design was notable for having air-operated twin sliding doors to facilitate passenger access and egress although there were no gangways.

In 1960 the GE lines were converted to 25 kV AC overhead (with 6.25 kV AC under low bridges in the London area until later boosted) and the sets were rebuilt to use this system, when they were classified AM6. The introduction of the TOPS scheme in 1969 saw the sets further reclassified 306. All were withdrawn by 1981.

BR (Eastleigh) Standard Mark 1 1,500 V DC Overhead, later 25 kV AC/6.25 kV AC Overhead Outer Suburban Class 307 (Class AM7) Three-car EMUs

The Class 307s were the first 1,500 V DC overhead EMUs built to the original BR Mark 1 design, essentially an overhead pick-up version of the 750 V DC 3rd rail SR 2-EPB design of 1953, which had been the first multiple unit to employ the new standard coach. BR's Eastleigh works built thirty-two sets in 1956 for the Great Eastern's Liverpool Street–Southend (Victoria) outer suburban services. They had two-class accommodation but no gangways. In 1960 the Southend line was converted to the 25 kV/6.25 kV AC overhead system and the Class 507s were modified accordingly in 1960–62. Some were later used on the LT&S lines out of Fenchurch Street.

The sets were extensively refurbished in the 1980s and gangways were fitted within each set. The cab front was also modified, the headcode panel being plated up. In 1991 the few survivors were transferred to the West Yorkshire PTE, where they lasted until 1993. A plan to convert withdrawn sets to Class 300 mail/parcels units was abandoned in favour of building the Class 325s. A departmental conversion to a test bed for three phase 'Holec' AC motors (as Class 316) survived until 2006.

BR (York) Standard Mark 1 25 kV AC Overhead Outer/Inner Suburban Class 308 (Class AM8) Three- and Four-car EMUs

The Class AM8 (later Class 308) EMUs were of standard BR Mark 1 (1959) design and were essentially an updated Class 302 design with the new 1959 standard sloping cab front, more modern electrical equipment and, after refurbishment, within-set gangways. All were built at BR's York works in 1961 for the ER Great Eastern Line's 25 kV AC system. The thirty-three Class 308/1 four-car sets were for Liverpool Street–Colchester–Clacton/Walton-on-the-Naze outer suburban and semi-fast services, although towards the end of their lives they were transferred to the LT&S line.

Passing Bethnal Green on its way to Liverpool Street is BR (ER)/LNER inner suburban Class 306 (or Class AM6) three-car EMU No. 083, September 1976.

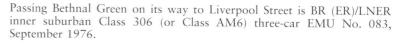

BR (ER) Class 307 (or Class AM7) four-car outer suburban EMU. No. 307 123 (ex-No. 123) in rail blue and grey livery surmounting Bethnal Green Bank on a Liverpool Street–Shenfield–Southend (Victoria) service, September 1982.

Preserved at the Electric Railway Museum on 10 September 2011 is Class 307 (or Class AM7) Driving Trailer Brake Second of outer suburban three-car EMU No. 307 123 (originally No. 123).

The nine Class 308/2 non-gangwayed four-car sets were for the L&TS's Fenchurch Street–Tilbury route to link with ocean liner services and unusually included a MLV (Motor Luggage Van) within its formation. However, the MLV became a luxury that was no longer needed with changing traffic patterns, so in 1971 the MLVs were converted to MBSs (Motor Brake Seconds). Further, with the cessation of the liner trade at Tilbury in 1983, all the Class 308/2s were withdrawn but three were converted to three-car parcels units and reclassified 308/4s.

The last subclass was the three Class 308/3 non-gangwayed sets, which differed from the other subclasses in that they were three-car inner suburban units with second-class-only accommodation; they were for the Liverpool Street–Enfield and Chingford routes. In 1993 the Class 308/1s, by then the only members of Class 308 in service, were reformed as three-car standard-class-only sets and transferred to the West Midlands and West Yorkshire PTEs. The last set was withdrawn in 2001.

Above: BR (ER) Class 308/1 (or Class AM8/1) outer suburban four-car EMU No. 154 (later No. 308 154) passing Bethnal Green on its way to Liverpool Street, September 1976.

Left: Passing Bethnal Green on a Liverpool Street–Chingford service in September 1982 is Class 308/3 (or Class AM8/3) inner suburban three-car EMU No. 308 455 (ex-No. 455) in rail blue and grey livery.

BR (York) Standard Mark 1 25 kV AC Overhead Clacton Express Class 309 (Class AM9) Two-, Three- and Four-car EMUs

The Class 309s (or AM9s) were built in 1962–63 by BR's York works for the 25 kV AC overhead GEML Liverpool St.–Colchester–Clacton/Walton-on-the-Naze express services. With two-class accommodation, the 309s were of standard BR Mark 1 express design and had gangways within sets and in the cabs for communication between sets. They had Commonwealth bogies and were the first EMUs to have a 100-mph maximum speed.

The eight Class 309/1s were built as two-car units (later strengthened to three, then four cars in 1977–80, two being reclassified 309/4); the eight Class 309/2s were four-car sets with a griddle/buffet car but this was removed in 1980, reducing the sets to three cars, although eventually they were strengthened to four cars. In 1993, seven were transferred to the north-west for Manchester services. The seven Class 309/3s were also four-car sets, but without eating facilities. All were withdrawn from GEML services in 1994, but seven went to the north-west to work Manchester Piccadilly–Crewe–Stoke-on-Trent (and occasionally Birmingham New Street) services until they, too, were withdrawn in 2000, although two sets saw departmental use as three-car Class 960 sets until 2004.

BR (Eastleigh) Bulleid 750 V DC 3rd Rail Outer Suburban Class 402 (SR Class 2-HAL) Two-car EMUs

The 2-HAL's were originally designed by OVS Bulleid for the Southern Railway (South Eastern Division) outer suburban and main line semi-fast services on the 750 V DC 3rd rail Victoria–Maidstone/Gillingham lines and therefore had two-class accommodation. The original

seventy-seven units, built in 1938–39, had hybrid Bulleid/Maunsell features, employing mixed steel/wood construction with domed cabs. They were built at Eastleigh on frames built at Lancing. A further sixteen similar units followed in 1940 for the South Western Division's Waterloo–Aldershot/Reading line.

Following war losses, Bulleid completely revised the design and in 1948, under British Railways management, introduced six sets which bore little relationship to the early sets; the revised design was more an outer suburban version of the contemporary 4-SUBs (Class 405) with slab cab fronts and the typical Bulleid curved coach side profile. Being of all-steel build, the post-war units were nicknamed 'Tin Hals'. Curiously, and very late in the day, another single unit was produced in 1955 as an accident replacement at a time when the design was obsolete and when it would have been more logical to have built a version of the more modern Bulleid 2-EPB – construction of such a version did, in fact, begin the following year in the shape of the Class 414/1 2-HAPs which were intended to replace the 2-HALs!

As with the 2-HAPs, many 2-HALs had their first-class accommodation downgraded to second as they got older and gravitated to less important services, but oddly they were not reclassified as the 2-HAPs were. The last 2-HALs were withdrawn in 1971 but six sets were converted to 2-PAN parcels/newspapers units, although they survived only another year.

BR (Eastleigh) Bulleid 750 V DC 3rd Rail Inner Suburban Class 405 (SR Class 4-SUB) Four-car EMUs

The Class 4-SUB was Bulleid's design for inner suburban services on the Southern Railway and 127 sets were built at Eastleigh (using frames built at Lancing). Two prototypes were built in 1941 and 1944

BR (ER) Class 309/1 (or Class AM9/1) express three-car EMU No. 601 (later No. 309 601) in rail blue and grey at Liverpool Street, March 1985. The Class 309/1 sets were built as two-car units but later strengthened to three, then four cars in 1977–80.

Class 309/2 (or Class AM9/2) express four-car EMU No. 617 (later No. 309 617) entering Liverpool Street, August 1982.

BR Class 402 (SR 2-HAL) two-car outer suburban EMU No. 2698 at East Croydon on a Bognor Regis–Victoria service, 17 March 1964. The 2-HAL is likely to have been attached to the front at Gatwick Airport. Although photographed after the introduction of yellow warning panels, the front end of the green-liveried set is devoid of such embellishment. (Photograph courtesy of Robert Carroll)

BR Class 405/2 (SR 4-SUB) four-car inner suburban EMUs, Nos. 4707 and 4685 on an Alton–Waterloo service in the outer London suburbs, May 1975.

Leaving Victoria on a Victoria–Streatham Common–West Croydon–Epsom Downs service is BR Class 405/2 (SR 4-SUB) four-car EMU No. 4732 repainted in Southern Railway malachite-green livery, but with a contemporary all-yellow front end, August 1982.

with domed front ends and, although designed to have two-class accommodation, entered service with third class (second from 1956) only. Eight production sets followed in 1945, designed from scratch for third class only – the first such EMUs on the Southern to do so and a precursor of what was to come on many EMUs and DMUs on British Railways' suburban and local services.

Further production sets followed with new slab fronts, to be designated under TOPS Class 405/1 (fifty-three built 1946–48) or 405/2 (sixty-four built 1948–51 with improved traction motors). It is also notable that, whilst the early sets followed the all-compartment layout, the 1946 batch featured semi-open motor coaches to be followed from 1948 by batches (ten 405/1s and all 405/2s) with three out of four cars fully open; in the early 1980s even the compartment trailers in surviving sets were replaced with open vehicles from withdrawn sets and several reformations of units took place. No gangways were fitted. Almost all sets featured stencil headcodes but seven trialled roller blinds which were adopted on later SR EMUs. The last 4-SUB was withdrawn in 1983.

BR (Eastleigh) Bulleid 750 V DC 3rd Rail Inner Suburban Class 4-DD Four-car EMUs

A unique design for the UK was Oliver Bulleid's Class 4-DD double-decker inner suburban four-car EMU for the Southern Railway, although by the time the two experimental sets were delivered in 1949 from Eastleigh, it was to the Southern Region of the newly nationalised British Railways. The 750 V DC, 3rd rail sets were always coupled together and were used only on the Charing Cross–Dartford service, which was one of the most heavily congested on the busy SR system.

The 4-DDs were typical of Bulleid's ability to 'think outside the box' – brilliant, yet flawed. A double-decker train would normally be well outside the British loading gauge, so what Bulleid did was design what was really a 'one and a half decker'! The upper and lower compartments were arranged 'en echelon', with entry to the upper seats being by steps from the lower compartment – there was no separate access to the upper one. Unfortunately, this resulted in longer dwell times at stations which counteracted the greater carrying capacity of the sets; the resultant delays had a knock-on effect on other services. Moreover, the lack of internal corridors or gangways within the sets meant passengers, once boarded, could not move to a possibly less congested area. Also, the upper compartments, which did not have opening windows because of restricted clearances, became very stuffy, which the advanced pressure ventilation system failed to alleviate. In addition, the lack of footboards adjacent to the lower compartment doors (again because of restricted clearances) resulted in several accidents to passengers boarding or alighting.

Despite all the problems of the 4-DDs – which resulted in the SR deciding to lengthen platforms to cater for longer trains instead – the two sets remained in traffic until 1971 and they proved very reliable. Although withdrawn before the TOPS classification was introduced, I have often speculated whether the vacant Class 406 – next to the Class 405 4-SUBs – was to be allocated to them when the TOPS system was under preparation. Perhaps someone knows?

Recently withdrawn BR (SR) Class 4-DD inner suburban four-car double-decker EMU No. 4902 (originally No. 4002) in rail blue at Ashford Works, October 1972.

BR (Eastleigh) Standard Mark 1 750 V DC 3rd Rail Express Class 410 and 412 (SR Class 4-BEP) and Class 411 (SR Class 4-CEP) Four-car EMUs and Class 411 (Class 3-CEP) Three-car EMUs

These classes have a complex history. The 4-CEPs (TOPS Class 411s) and the buffet-equipped 4-BEPs (Class 410s) were the first main line express EMUs to be based on the standard BR Mark 1 coach design. Naturally, they had first- and second-class accommodation and were gangwayed both within and between sets. They were built at BR Eastleigh (with frames built at Ashford) in 1956–57 (the prototypes tested on the SR's Central Division before transfer to the South Eastern Division's Kent services), 1958–59 (for the Kent Coast electrification Phase 1), 1960–61 (for the Kent Coast electrification Phase 2) and 1963 (for the South Western Division but soon transferred to the South Eastern Division).

The prototypes (fitted with 1951 electrical equipment) were classified 410/1 (two 4-BEP sets) and 411/1 (four 4-CEP sets) and the production sets (with 1957 equipment) 410/2 (ten 4-BEP Phase 1 and ten 4-BEP Phase 2 sets) and 411/2 (forty-nine 4-CEP Phase 1 and fifty-eight 4-CEP Phase 2 sets). The 4-CEPs and some 4-BEPs were refurbished by BREL Eastleigh (1975: a prototype Class 411/3 4-CEP) and Swindon (1979–84: five Class 411/4 and 116 Class 411/5 4-CEP sets including eight converted from 4-BEPs with the buffet car replaced with a standard trailer; and seven 412/3 4-BEP sets).

During the refurbishment programme, four Class 482/7 4-TEP units were formed in 1982, each of three cars from a refurbished 4-CEP and an non-refurbished buffet car from a 4-BEP for the London–Hastings route, but all were disbanded by 1986 when the cars were reformed into standard refurbished 4-CEPs. Six sets were temporarily reduced by BR to three-car sets in 1993–94 as Class 411/6 3-CEPs. In the late 1990s three Connex South Central Class 411/5s 4-CEPs were fitted with high speed Mk.6 bogies and used the same (now vacant) 411/6 classification. South West Trains reduced twenty of their 411/5s to three-car 3-CEP sets in 1999–2005, reclassifying them 411/9.

In 2002, South West Trains reformed several sets in a rather curious way when the buffet cars were taken from the seven Class 412/3 4-BEPs to replace a saloon car in seven 4-CEPs, which then took up the classification 412/2 (4-BEP). The displaced saloons were inserted into the seven Class 412/3 4-BEPs which thus effectively became 4-CEPs, although, confusingly, they retained the 412 classification (412/1) rather than the 411 of CEPs! Apparently, the 4-BEPs had better acceleration than a 4-CEP so the 412/1s had the high acceleration of a BEP coupled with the greater seating capacity of a CEP. Both the 4-CEPs and 4-BEPs were mostly withdrawn in the 2002–05 period.

BR (Eastleigh) Standard Mark 1 and Bulleid 750 V DC 3rd Rail Outer Suburban Class 414 (SR Class 2-HAP) Two-car EMUs

The SR's 209 Class 2-HAP sets were of two distinct designs. One design used the recovered frames from withdrawn 2-NOL units which were fitted with new bodies of Bulleid pattern (as the current standard BR Mark 1 coach bodies would not fit the frames) at Eastleigh. These thirty-six sets were put into service in 1956–58 (414/1) on the Thanet services of the South Eastern Division.

Parallel to the construction of the Bulleid Class 414/1s, the BR Mark 1 body was used in sets built by BR in Eastleigh in 1957 with 1951 electro-pneumatic control equipment (forty-two Class 414/2 sets) and,

Above left: BR Class 411/2 (SR Class 4-CEP) express four-car EMU No. 7139 in rail blue and grey livery at Charing Cross, May 1975.

Above right: Speeding past Longfield on a Dover–Chatham–Herne Hill–Victoria service is BR Class 411/5 (SR Class 4-CEP) four-car EMU No. 411 515, August 1984.

Left: Preserved at the Pontypool & Blaenavon Railway is Class 411/9 (Class 3-CEP) three-car EMU No. (41)1198; pictured at Blaenavon depot, 18 September 2011. This set was converted from a Class 412/1 (a 4-BEP with a saloon instead of a buffet!) No. (41)2314 which in turn had been reformed from a refurbished Class 412/3 4-BEP No. (41)2304. No. 1198 was repainted into the 'heritage' livery of rail blue for use by South West Trains on the Lymington branch in 1999–2005.

with the improved 1957 camshaft control system, in 1958–63 (131 Class 414/3 sets) for outer suburban and main line semi-fast services and therefore had two-class accommodation. Initially, they were used on the newly electrified Kent Coast route of the South Eastern Division and also on the South Western and Central Divisions of the Southern Region.

Many of both Bulleid and BR Mark 1 2-HAPs were transferred to the South West Division and reclassified Class 418 2-SAP when their first-class accommodation was downgraded to second (twelve Class 414/1 sets to class 418/0 in 1969; forty-two Class 414/2 to 418/1 in 1973; and one Class 414/3 to 418/2 in 1973). However, because of further stock reallocations, first class was restored in 1970 (414/1) and 1979–80 (414/2 and 3) and the 2-SAPs regained their former classification. But then the Class 414/1s were again reduced to Class 418 2-SAPs in 1976 when moved to the Central Section suburban services.

In 1982–91 many BR Mark 1 Class 414/2 and 3 2-HAP sets were semi-permanently coupled together to form thirteen Class 413/2 (1951 equipment) and sixteen Class 413/3 (1957 equipment) 4-CAP four-car sets for the Coastaway service. The last 4-CAPs were withdrawn in 1995. The last Bulleid 2-SAPs were withdrawn in 1982–83 whilst the last BR Mark 1 2-HAP was withdrawn in 1984, although in 1985 ten were converted into individual Gatwick luggage vans for use in loco-hauled Gatwick Express trains.

Right top: BR Class 414/2 (SR Class 2-HAP) outer suburban two-car EMU No. 6013 at Waterloo, March 1984.

Right bottom: No fewer than five two-car EMUs pass Longfield on a Charing Cross–Margate service with, at the rear, Class 414/3 (SR Class 2-HAP) No. 6096, August 1984.

BR (Eastleigh) Standard Mark 1 and Bulleid 750 V DC 3rd Rail Inner Suburban Class 415 (SR Class 4-EPB) Four-car EMUs

The Class 415/1s were a development of the Class 405 4-SUBs with improved power/control equipment including electro-pneumatic brakes and electro-contactor control equipment, being known as 1951 stock. They also had roller-blind headcodes, previously trialled on a small number of 4-SUBs. As with the 4-SUBs, they had all third- (later second-) class accommodation and no gangways. The 4-EPBs (415/1s) were first proposed by the Southern Railway on the eve of nationalisation but were not built until 1951–57 by BR Eastleigh, still to Bulleid's body profile as the standard BR Mark 1 design had not yet been developed. In total, 213 sets were constructed (fifty-three in 1951–54 with Eastern Division bogies and 160 in 1953–57 with Central Division bogies).

Unlike the Bulleid Class 415/1s, the seventy 415/2 sets were built to the standard BR Mk.1 design in 1960–63 (fifty-six sets in 1960 for the Eastern and Central Divisions and fourteen sets in 1962–63 for the South Western Division). Although many 4-EPBs were withdrawn in the 1980s, those remaining in service were extensively refurbished. The 415/1s were refurbished from 1980 and reclassified 415/4, and the 415/2s from 1982, when they were reclassified 415/6 or, when re-geared for 90 mph, 415/7. The Class 415/5 constituted stock of both Bulleid and Mark 1 designs which consolidated the to-be-phased-out compartment cars for limited service in the 1980s until withdrawal. They were also reclassified 4-COM. The last 4-EPBs, of both Bulleid and Mark 1 design, were withdrawn in 1995.

BR (Eastleigh) Standard Mark 1 and Bulleid 750 V DC 3rd Rail Inner Suburban Class 416 (SR Class 2-EPB) Two-car EMUs

As with the 4-EPBs, the two-car variety was of two distinct designs. The earliest to appear were the 416/2s built to the standard BR Mark 1 design. The first batch of seventy-nine sets were built in 1953–54 at Eastleigh (with frames built at Ashford and Lancing) for the South Eastern Division of the Southern Region. The second batch of fifteen sets were built at Eastleigh in 1955 (with larger brake vans and two class seating) originally for the NER's 600 V DC 3rd rail South Tyneside service but when that route was de-electrified, the sets were modified (including the declassification of first class) for transfer to the South Western Division in 1963.

The second 2-EPB design (later classified 416/1) was the first SR sets with all open saloon seating when delivered from BR's Eastleigh works in 1959. They were built to Bulleid's body profile rather than the standard BR Mk.1 profile; this was because they used salvaged 2-NOL frames onto which BR bodies could not be fitted. They were originally classified 2-NOP but this changed later to 2-EPB. The 416/1s were refurbished in 1983 and reclassified 416/3; and the 416/2s in 1986 when they became 416/4. Some of the 416/3s were later transferred to the North London line. The last 2-EPBs were withdrawn in 1995, although some survived in departmental use until 2005.

Above: BR inner suburban Class 415/1 (SR Class 4-EPB) four-car EMU No. 5245 (with a Class 416/2 2-EPB) in rail blue livery, crossing Charing Cross Bridge, July 1975. This particular set unusually had two compartment trailer seconds rather than the usual one compartment and one open second.

Right: Pictured is Class 415/1 (SR Class 4-EPB) four-car EMU No. 5043 at Charing Cross, July 1975.

Speeding past Longfield is Class 415/1 (SR Class 4-EPB) four-car EMU No. 5232 in rail blue and grey livery, August 1984.

Refurbished Class 415/4 (SR Class 4-EPB) four-car EMU No. 5452 at Redhill, August 1986.

BR Class 416/1 (SR Class 2-EPB) inner suburban two-car EMU No. 5669 in rail blue livery having just arrived at Charing Cross on a Dartford loop service, May 1975.

Approaching Teddington on a Waterloo–Shepperton service in May 1975 is Class 416/2 (SR Class 2-EPB) two-car EMU No. 5756 (with 416/1 Nos 5680 and 5682).

BR (Eastleigh) Standard Mark 1 and Bulleid 750 V DC 3rd Rail Outer Suburban Class 418 (SR Class 2-SAP) Two-car EMUs

The 2-SAPs were converted from 2-HAPs of standard BR Mark 1 design built by BR in Eastleigh in 1957 (414/2 with 1951 equipment) and 1958–63 (414/3 with 1957 equipment) or of SR Bulleid pattern built in 1956–58 (414/1) for outer suburban or main line semi-fast services with first-class accommodation – which was downgraded during the conversion to 2-SAPs.

Twelve Bulleid Class 414/1 sets were converted to 418/0 in 1969, forty-three BR Mk.1 sets in 1973 (forty-two 414/2s to 418/1 and one Class 414/3 to a 418/2) when transferred to the South West Division. However, because of further stock reallocations, first class was restored in 1970 (414/1) and 1979–80 (414/2 and 3) and the 2-SAPs regained their former 2-HAP classification. But then the Class 414/1 2-HAPs were again reduced to Class 418/0 2-SAPs in 1976 when moved to the Central Section suburban services. The last Bulleid 2-SAPs were withdrawn in 1982–83.

BR (Eastleigh) Standard Mark 1 750 V DC 3rd Rail Motor Luggage Van Class 419 (SR Class MLV) and Trailer Luggage Van Class 499 (SR Class TLV) Single Cars

Ten MLVs of BR Mark 1 design were built by BR, Eastleigh, in 1959 and 1961 to be attached to the SR's South Eastern Division's boat trains (composed of two 4-CEPs and a 4-BEP) from Victoria to Dover Western Docks and Folkestone. The MLVs also had batteries for working in sidings which were not electrified. The design was based on a single MLV (without batteries) built in 1955 at Eastleigh for the South

Tyneside 600 V DC network, although when that was de-electrified in 1963 the MLV was transferred to the LMR's Southport–Liverpool 650 V DC line before withdrawal in 1968.

To work with the MLVs, in 1968 BR's Eastleigh works converted six loco-hauled full brakes into TLVs (Trailer Luggage Vans), TOPS Class 499. However, declining boat-train traffic saw them taken out of service in 1975, although they survived in departmental traffic, the last not being withdrawn until 2011. The SR's MLVs lasted in full service much longer, not being withdrawn until 1991–92, though again, they survived in departmental service as Class 931 tractor units, the last going in 2004.

BR/BREL (York) Standard Mark 1 750 V DC 3rd Rail Express Class 420 and 422 (SR Class 4-BIG) and Class 421 (SR 4-CIG) Four-car EMUs

The buffet-equipped 4-BIGs (TOPS Class 420s) were of standard BR Mark 1 design as were the 4-CIGs (Class 421s), which did not include a buffet car. They were effectively an updated, cleaned-up version of the earlier 4-BEPs/CEPs and likewise had two-class accommodation with gangways throughout. The two classes were built by BR, York in two phases: in 1964–66 (thirty-six 4-CIGs Phase 1; 421/1) and 1965–66 (eighteen 4-BIG Phase 1; 420/1) for London Bridge/Victoria–Brighton and South Coast services; and 1970–72 (102 4-CIG Phase 2; 421/2) and 1970 (ten 4-BIG Phase 2 420/2) for Waterloo–Portsmouth services.

Aside from two temporary formations of Class 421/0 8-MIGs (a 4-CIG + buffet car + 3-CIG) in the summer of 1983, there were several modification and refurbishment programmes. Looking firstly at 4-CIGs, BR refurbished fifty-three Class 421/1s Phase 1 4-CIGs in 1986–93 and

Above left: In June 1975, BR Class 418/2 (SR Class 2-SAP) outer suburban two-car EMU No. 5908 passes Mortlake on its way to Waterloo.

Above right: Class 418/1 (SR Class 2-SAP) two-car EMU No. 5942 is seen just after leaving Whitton and branching off the Windsor–Reading line to Hounslow and Brentford on its way to Waterloo, April 1975.

Right: BR Class 419 (SR Class MLV) rail motor luggage van No. 68006 (later No. [41]9006) in rail blue and grey at Victoria, July 1975.

Above: BR Class 420/1 (SR Class 4-BIG) express four-car EMU No. 7037 (with a 4-CIG) in rail blue and grey livery nearing Victoria, September 1976.

Right: Pulling into Portsmouth Harbour in August 1986 is Class 421/2 (SR Class 4-CIG) four-car EMU No. 7339.

eighty-seven Class 421/2 Phase 2 4-CIGs in 1987–93 and reclassified them Class 421/3 and 421/4 respectively. In 1990–92 BR fitted twenty-two 4-CIGs with modifications to improve their performance and reclassified these 'Greyhound' sets 421/5; in 1999 South West Trains fitted eight 4-BIG sets with these improvements and at the same time replaced their buffets with a 4-CEP saloon, reclassifying them Class 421/8 4-CIGs. The eight 421/6s were Phase 1 4-CIGs fitted with Mk.6 bogies by BR in 1990–92. In 1997, eleven withdrawn 4-BIGs were completely rebuilt and their buffet cars removed for use on the Brighton–Portsmouth Coastaway route, being reclassified 421/7 3-COP, although a trailer was later added and they became 4-COP. Confusingly, in 2004, three Class 421/4 4-CIGs were reduced to 3-CIGs for use on the Lymington branch and also classed as 421/7.

As for the 4-BIG refurbishment programme in which the buffets were retained, ten Class 420/1 Phase 1s were refurbished in 1985–86 and reclassified 422/1s, then ten Class 420/2 Phase 2s in 1986–88 as 422/2s. In 1989, twelve of these refurbished 4-BIGs of both Phase 1 and 2 sets were refitted with Mk.6 power bogies as 422/3. In 1992, four Class 422/0 8-DIG sets were formed by semi-permanently coupling a 4-CIG and 4-BIG and fitting them with Mk.6 bogies for the Capital Coast Express operated by Connex South Central. As for withdrawal, the last 4-BIGs (422/3s) went in 1989, the last 4-CIGs (421/8s) in 1999 and the 3-CIGs (421/7s) in 2004–05.

BR/BREL (York) Standard Mark 1 750 V DC 3rd Rail Outer Suburban/Semi-fast Class 423 (SR Class 4-VEP) Four-car EMUs

The 194 4-VEP (TOPS Class 423) sets were of standard BR Mark 1 design – essentially a high-density version of the 4-CIGs – and built by BR and BREL in York 1967–74 for outer suburban and main line semi-fast services on all three sections of the Southern Region. They had two-class accommodation and – a first for outer suburban Southern EMUs – gangways throughout.

When the 4-VEPs were facelifted in 1988–96, the non-refurbished sets became 423/0 and the 191 refurbished ones 423/4, soon being changed to 423/1. In 1967 the Bournemouth line was electrified but a shortage of stock soon became apparent and the following year a temporary 8-VAB set (Class 480) was formed, composed of cars from three standard sets plus a former loco-hauled buffet. The set was disbanded in 1974 when sufficient 4-REPs were delivered.

In 1998–99 Connex South Central converted nineteen sets into inner suburban Class 423/2 (later 423/9) 4-VOP sets (without first-class accommodation or toilets) to work the South London line between Victoria and London Bridge, although in 2003, eight 4-VOPs were reformed with a driving trailer composite (retaining its first class accommodation) from a 4-VEP, the resulting hybrid being known as a 4-VIP (Class 423/8), so as to be available to work other services. The last of the 4-VEP/VIP/VOPs were withdrawn in 2004–05.

BR/BREL (York) Standard Mark 1 750 V DC 3rd Rail Gatwick Express Class 427 SR (Class 4-VEG) Four-car EMUs

In 1978 twelve 4-VEPs were converted into Class 427 4-VEG (with extra luggage capacity) as dedicated units for the Gatwick Express service. When they were displaced by Class 73 electro-diesel locos and standard BR Mk.3 coaches in 1984, the 4-VEG were converted back into 4-VEPs.

Above left: BR Class 423/0 (SR Class 4-VEP) outer suburban four-car EMU No. 7885, later no. (42)3185, in rail blue and grey awaiting departure at Victoria for Dover Priory, July 1975.

Above right: Seen departing Victoria is Class 423/1 (SR Class 4-VEP) four-car EMU No. 7810, later no. (42)3110, April 1984.

Left: BR Class 427 (SR 4-VEG) Gatwick Express four-car EMU No. 7907 in rail blue and grey with 'Rapid City Link Gatwick–London' branding, departing Victoria for its destination of Gatwick Airport, August 1982.

BR/BREL (York) Standard Mark 1 750 V DC 3rd Rail Express Tractor Class 441/430/432 (SR Class 4-REP) Four-car EMUs

When the Bournemouth line was electrified, the extension on to Weymouth was unfortunately not. As a result, the SR decided to use formations comprising a very high powered 'tractor' 4-REP unit with one or two trailer TC sets; on arrival at Bournemouth, the one or two TCs would detach from the 4-REP and continue to Weymouth hauled by a Class 33/1 locomotive as a push-pull working. The opposite arrangements occurred in the other direction. The two-class, buffet-equipped, gangwayed 4-REPs consisted of eleven Phase 1 sets built by BR, York in 1966–67, composed of new-build driving motors with trailers converted from loco-hauled standard BR Mk.1 stock; and four Phase 2 sets built by BREL, York, in 1974, all cars of which were newly built.

The sets were initially classified as 441 under TOPS, which was then changed to 430, although at the end of their lives they were reclassified as 432. Withdrawal of the 4-REPs began in 1988 so their motors could be reused in the Class 442s, but the need for stock on the newly electrified South Hampshire Line resulted, in 1990, in the formation of four 6-REP sets made up of redundant REP/TC cars; they also served on the Weymouth line as an interim measure until all the new Class 442 (5-WES) sets were delivered. The last 4/6-REPs were withdrawn in 1991, although some individual cars lasted in departmental use until 2012.

BR/BREL (York) Standard Mark 1 Express Trailer Class 442/491/438 (SR Class 4-TC) Four-car MUs and Class 442/492 (SR Class 3-TC) Three-car MUs

The SR's electrification of the Waterloo–Bournemouth line in 1967 did not extend to Weymouth, which was not thought to be justified at the time. As stated previously, the SR decided to use formations of a 'tractor' 4-REP with one- or two-trailer TC sets which, at Bournemouth, would be detached from the 4-REP and be coupled to a push-pull fitted Class 33/1 locomotive for the onward journey to Weymouth. In the reverse direction, the opposite applied. Occasionally, the TCs worked on other services, such as Waterloo–Salisbury, hauled by a loco rather than a 4-REP.

Following a 6-TC prototype composed of old Maunsell EMU cars formed in 1965, twenty-eight gangwayed 4-TCs and three 3-TCs were converted from standard BR Mk.1 loco-hauled stock in 1966–67 by BR, York, as Phase 1 units. In 1974, three new 4-TCs were converted from loco-hauled stock as Phase 2 units; in addition, the 3-TCs were eventually strengthened to 4-TCs.

The TOPS classification of these sets is rather confusing. At first (1972), 4-TCs were classed 442/1 and the 3-TCs 442/2 but they were subsequently reclassified to Class 491 and 492 respectively. However, towards the end of their life (when all were 4-TCs) they were reclassified 438. In 1986, two sets were converted to include a buffet car as 4-TCBs (492/8) and then modified, together with another four sets, for trolley service only as 4-TCTs (438/1), whilst in 1988, three sets became 5-TCBs (438/9) for a short time, as by the end of the year all sets were withdrawn.

Above: BR Class 430 (SR Class 4-REP) express four-car EMU No. 3007 departing Waterloo on a Weymouth service, pushing two 4-TC sets, March 1984.

Right: BR Class 491 (SR Class 4-TC) express four-car trailer MU No. 421 about to depart Waterloo on a Weymouth service, March 1984.

BR (Eastleigh) Standard Mark 1 630 V DC 3rd Rail Inner Suburban London District Class 501 Three-car EMUs

The fifty-seven Class 501s were built by BR, Eastleigh, (with frames constructed at Ashford) in 1957–58 for the LMR's 630 V DC 3rd rail (originally four rails) London District inner suburban services, namely Broad Street–Richmond/Watford and Euston–Watford services. Originally, in accordance with LMR policy, only individual cars were numbered but when the cars were refurbished in the 1980s set numbers under the TOPS system were introduced. The class was of standard BR Mark 1 design, essentially a short-framed version of the SR's EPB EMUs. No gangways were fitted. The Class 501 sets were withdrawn in 1988, although three sets, reduced to two cars (Class 936), saw departmental use into the 2000s.

LMS (Derby) 650 V DC 3rd Rail Inner Suburban Liverpool Northern Class 502 Two-, Three- and Five-car EMUs

The fifty-eight sets were built by the Derby works of the LMS for their Liverpool Northern line (Liverpool Exchange–Southport/Ormskirk) 650 V DC 3rd rail suburban services in 1939. They were a longer, wider version of the LMS's Wirral line stock (Class 503), sharing the same very modern styling with sliding doors and were of integral construction without a separate frame. Unusually, they were built as either a self-contained three-car unit (thirty-four sets) with a driving car at each end or a two-car unit (twenty-four sets) with a driving car only at one end; these latter sets could not operate independently of a three-car set, thus forming a five-car set.

The Class 502s were built with first- and third-class (second class from 1956) accommodation but they became all second class in the late 1960s. Unlike the Class 503s, the 502s retained their triple-window cab until withdrawal (in 1981) because they did not work in the Mersey Tunnels and therefore did not need a central emergency door. The 502s were also not multiplied by BR, unlike their Class 503 sisters, but since they were so closely related to the similar Class 503s and because they survived in BR service much longer (1978–80) than other pre-war built sets, a photo is included in this book. In accordance with LMS and LMR policy, they were never given set numbers. Moreover, the TOPS set numbers were never carried.

Metropolitan Cammell (Saltley) and Birmingham Railway Carriage & Wagon Co. (Smethwick) 650 V DC 3rd Rail Inner Suburban Wirral and Mersey Class 503 Three-car EMUs

The first batch of seventeen Class 503s were built by Metropolitan Cammell at their Saltley works and the Birmingham Railway Carriage & Wagon Co.'s Smethwick works for the LMS's Wirral and Mersey 650 V DC 3rd rail suburban network in 1938. A further batch of twenty-four (with four cars to replace cars destroyed in the war) with minor improvements was built in 1956–57 for BR (LMR). When the first sets appeared, their very modern styling with sliding doors was a huge contrast to other coaching and EMU stock of the period. They seem to have been influenced by the BRC&W's 'O' and 'P' underground stock for London Transport and were of integral construction.

The Class 503s had both first- and third-class (second class from 1956) accommodation (the former downgraded in the early 1970s). Originally they were constructed with three windows in the cab, but, as they worked in tunnels under central Liverpool, they were fitted with a central door for emergency access/exit in 1972. In accordance with LMS

BR (LMR) London District Class 501 inner suburban three-car EMU, later No. 501 168, in rail blue livery, awaiting departure at the now demolished Broad Street on a Watford service, May 1975. At this time, only the cars were given numbers – in this case Nos. M61168, M70168 and M75168.

Seen at the characterful Broad Street station is Class 501 London District three-car EMU, No. 169, later No. 501 169, livery having arrived at Broad Street on a service from Richmond, September 1982. Note that, although set numbers would have been allocated by this time, the only set number displayed is 169 in the miniature headcode panel in the window.

Just arrived at Broad Street on a service from Richmond is Class 501 London District three-car EMU No. 501 139 in rail blue and grey livery, September 1982.

BR (LMR)/LMS) Class 502 Liverpool Northern inner suburban five-car EMU made up of a three-car unit (car Nos M28330M, M29560M and M29873M) and a two-car set (car Nos. M28328M and M29872M) basks in the late autumn sunlight at Southport on a Liverpool Exchange service, November 1978.

Above left: BR (LMR)/LMS Wirral and Mersey Class 503 inner suburban three-car EMU, Nos. M29287M, M29717M, M28687M, in rail blue with Merseyrail branding at Birkenhead North on a West Kirby–Liverpool (Central)–Liverpool (St James) service, February 1978.

Above right: At Birkenhead North on a West Kirby–Liverpool (Central)–Liverpool (St James) service is rail blue Class 503 three-car EMU, Nos M28688M, M29710M, M29288M, with Merseyrail branding, February 1978.

Opposite: BR (LMR) Class 504 two-car inner suburban EMU, Nos. M77165 and M56444, in rail blue and grey livery with a Manchester PTE Metro logo nearing Manchester Victoria on a service from Bury, August 1982.

and LMR policy, they were never given set numbers. Under TOPS, it is believed that BR allocated them set numbers but, like some other LMR EMU classes, they were never carried. They were withdrawn in 1980–85.

BR (Wolverton) Standard Mark 1 1,200 V DC 3rd Rail Inner Suburban Class 504 Two-car EMUs

The Class 504s were the first standard BR Mark 1 design to have a revised cab and these and the following BR Mark 1 EMU classes were known as the 1959 design. Subsequent such designs (Classes 304, 305 and 308) had a four-character headcode panel above the cab. The twenty-six Class 504s were built in 1959 at Wolverton for the 1,200 V DC 3rd rail Manchester Victoria–Bury line, unique in having an enclosed side-contact system. Their accommodation was all second class and they had no gangways. The last sets were withdrawn in 1991 when the Bury line was converted to the Manchester Metrolink light rail/tram system. Like all LMR EMUs, the Class 504s did not carry set numbers before TOPS.

Metropolitan Cammell (Saltley) and Birmingham Railway Carriage & Wagon Co. (Smethwick) 1,500 V DC Overhead Inner Suburban Class 506 Three-car EMUs

The class were ordered by the LNER in 1938 from Metropolitan Cammell (Saltley) and the Birmingham Railway and Carriage Co. (Smethwick) for their planned 1,500 V DC overhead electrification of the Manchester Piccadilly–Glossop/Hadfield line. However, the Second World War delayed the construction of the sets until 1950 and they did not enter service until 1954 when the line was within BR's Eastern Region (although later the line was transferred to the London Midland Region).

The class was essentially a three-car version of the Class 306 (AM6) EMUs for the Great Eastern's Liverpool Street–Shenfield line. The Class 506 EMUs had sliding doors, but no gangways, and had both first and third (second from 1956) class accommodation until 1962 when they became mono-class. The introduction of the TOPS scheme in the early 1970s saw the units classified 306 (they did not previously have a specific classification), although they never carried the set numbers allocated them. They were withdrawn in 1984 when the line was converted to 25 kV AC.

Above left: BR (ER)/LNER Metro Cammell/BRCW Class 506 inner suburban three-car EMU, Nos M59406M, M59506M, M59606M (originally with E prefixes and suffixes) – Set No. 506 006 – in rail blue and grey livery with Manchester PTE logo departing Manchester (Piccadilly) on a service to Hadfield and Glossop, August 1982.

Above right: Departing Manchester (Piccadilly) on a service to Hadfield and Glossop in August 1982 is Class 506 three-car EMU Nos M59504M, M59504M, M59604M (originally with E prefixes and suffixes) – Set No. 506 004 – in rail blue and grey livery with Manchester PTE logo.

2

First Generation EMUs – Standard BR Mark 2 Designs 1965–77

BR (Derby) Standard Mark 2 25 kV AC Overhead Outer Suburban Class 310 (Class AM10) Four-car EMUs

The AM10 (or Class 310 under TOPS) EMUs were built by BR's Derby works in 1965–67 for the LMR's 25 kV AC overhead Euston outer suburban and main line semi-fast services between Euston, Birmingham, Manchester and Liverpool. They were the first EMU design based on the new standard BR Mark 2 coach of semi-integral construction and the AM10s had several advanced technical features. Their accommodation was a notable advance over previous EMU designs.

Fifty sets were constructed, with internal gangways and with two-class accommodation. Thirteen sets were reduced to three-car Class 310/1s for the Midlands, the remainder becoming Class 310/0, which were later transferred for service on the London, Tilbury and Southend Line. They were withdrawn in 2001–02, although one set, modified to a Class 960 dual-voltage departmental unit for test purposes, survived until 2007.

BREL (York) Standard Mark 2 25 kV AC Overhead Outer Suburban Class 312 (Class AM12) Four-car EMUs

The Class 312s were an updated version of the Class 310s (AM10s) and were built by BR's York works in 1975–77 for the ER's 25 kV AC Great Northern King's Cross–Welwyn Garden City/Royston services (twenty-six Class 312/0 sets); the ER's Great Eastern Liverpool Street–Southend (Victoria) and Liverpool Street–Colchester–Clacton/Walton services (nineteen Class 312/1 sets) and the LMR's West Midlands/ Birmingham area (four Class 312/2 sets) services. Later, all were allocated to the Great Eastern services out of Liverpool Street except for the Class 312/1s which went to the LT&S services out of Fenchurch Street, eventually to be joined by the Class 312/2s.

The Class 312s were the last EMUs based on the BR Standard Mk.2 bodyshell, and were the last with slam doors – a feature which contributed to their relatively early demise by 2003–04. Although they would have been allocated the classification AM12 pre-TOPS, they appeared after its introduction and were thus never officially Class AM12s, although sometimes known as that among enthusiasts.

Above left: BR (LMR) Class 310 (originally Class AM10) outer suburban four-car EMU No. 053 (later No. 310 053) in BR blue livery arriving at Euston on a service from Bletchley, September 1982.

Above right: Departing Euston on a Birmingham New Street service in September 1982 is Class 310 (Class AM10) four-car EMU No. 310 056 (originally No. 056) in rail blue and grey.

Right: BR (ER) Class 312/0 (or Class AM12/0) outer suburban four-car EMU No. 312 724 in rail blue and grey approaching Finsbury Park on its way to King's Cross, August 1982.

3

Early Second Generation EMUs – BR 1972 Designs 1971–81

BREL (York) 1972 Design 750 V DC 3rd Rail Inner Suburban Class 445 (SR 4-PEP) Four-car EMUs and Class 446 (SR 2-PEP) Two-car EMU

Two prototype 4-PEP four-car sets (TOPS Class 445) of what was to be the second generation of BR's EMUs were constructed to gain experience for a new standard design to replace SR 4-SUBs and 4-EPBs, whilst sister prototype 2-PEP (TOPS Class 446) – finished in unpainted aluminium – was intended for a replacement design for 2-EPBs. In addition, a wider application for replacement stock on other BR regions' 750 V DC 3rd rail and 25 kV AC overhead network was planned. In the event, this is exactly what occurred.

Earlier BR EMU designs were based on the standard BR Mk.1 or Mk.2 coach designs. In contrast, the PEP design was not based on any contemporary loco-hauled coach but was simply known as the 1972 design, although only the 2-PEP was delivered in that year, the two 4-PEPs having been completed the previous year. The 1972 design

was gangwayed within each set but the cabs had a connecting door for emergency use only, such as evacuation in tunnels. The primary difference between the Class 445s and 446s and the production Class 313, 314, 315, 507 and 508 were that the angled cab-front of the prototypes was replaced with an aesthetically less pleasing flat cab-front on the production classes, which also had only two sets of sliding doors each side on each TSO (Trailer Second Open) rather than three.

I was living in Teddington at the time of the PEPs' introduction and travelled on it once to see what the design was like. The acceleration and quietness were most impressive but I have to say I preferred the amply cushioned, high-back seats of the BR Mk.1 and SR Bulleid stock I normally travelled in, rather than the tube-like interior of the PEPs. Withdrawn from passenger use in 1976, the two 4-PEP sets survived in departmental use as Class 935 until scrapped in 1986 and 1990. In 1974, the 2-PEP had an additional trailer with pantograph inserted to form a 3-PEP (Class 920) for testing on the 25 kV AC overhead lines of the Eastern and Scottish Regions. It was scrapped in 1987.

BR Class 445 (SR Class 4-PEP) inner suburban four-car EMU prototype No. 4002 (with No. 4001 leading) in rail blue livery leaving Waterloo on a Hampton Court service, July 1975. Note that the second driving car of the leading set (No. 4001) was originally part of Class 446 (SR 2-PEP) two-car EMU No. 2001 which was in unpainted aluminium. This driving car had been swapped with one of the blue-painted driving cars of 4-PEP No. 4001.

BREL (York) 1972 Design 25 kV AC Overhead/750 V DC 3rd Rail Inner Suburban Class 313 Three-car EMUs

The first production second-generation EMUs developed from the Class 445 (or 4-PEP) prototype sets, the sixty-four Class 313/0 four-car sets mainly differed in being dual voltage (25 kV AC overhead and 750 V DC 3rd rail), in having slab cab-fronts rather than angled ones and with the TSOs having only two pairs of sliding doors each side rather than three. They were built by BREL, York, in 1976–77 for the ER's newly electrified Great Northern line's Moorgate–Drayton Park–Welwyn Garden City/Hertford North service.

Subsequently, several sets were transferred temporarily to the Merseyrail network in the late 1970s and more for short periods to the Great Eastern's Colchester–Clacton/Walton line in the 1980s. Later still, sixteen sets went to the LMR's DC North London line (Richmond–Stratford), West London line (Willesden Jct.–Clapham Jct.) and Watford line (Euston–Watford Jct.) whilst one went to Network Rail, being reclassified 313/1. Further moves have resulted in nineteen units having their pantographs removed for working Southern's Coastaway lines and reclassification as 313/2 in 2010.

BREL (York) 1972 Design 25 kV AC Overhead Inner Suburban Class 314 Three-car EMUs

In 1979 sixteen Class 314s were built at York by BREL for the ScR as a single voltage (25 kV AC) version of the ER's Class 313s for Glasgow's inner suburban system. Two groups were built with differing traction motors.

BREL (York) 1972 Design 25 kV AC Overhead Inner Suburban Class 315 Four-car EMUs

The Class 315 was essentially a four-car, single-voltage version of the Class 313 and the last EMU class built to the 1972 design. BREL (York) completed sixty-one sets in 1980–81 to replace Class 306s on the ER's 25 kV AC Liverpool Street–Shenfield service, although later they spread to other Great Eastern services such as those on the Lea Valley line.

BREL (York) 1972 Design 750 V DC 3rd Rail Inner Suburban Class 507 Three-car EMUs

The Class 507s were the second class developed from the 4-PEP Class 445s to be put into production and thirty-three three-car sets were built by BREL, York, in 1978–80, specifically for the 750 V DC 3rd rail Merseyrail network to replace the LMS Class 502s.

BREL (York) 1972 Design 750 V DC 3rd Rail Inner Suburban Class 508 Three- and Four-car EMUs

The first production second-generation EMUs to be delivered to the Southern Region following the Class 445 (or 4-PEP) prototype trailers, the Class 508/0 four-car EMUs had been intended for the London Midland Region's Merseyside 750 V DC 3rd rail network (and had a lowered roof line to fit into the system's tunnels), but the urgent need of the Southern Region to replace ageing Bulleid 4-SUB sets resulted in them being allocated to the SR's south-west section.

Above: Seen north of Finsbury Park on a Hertford North–Moorgate service is BR (ER) Class 313/0 inner suburban three-car EMU No. 313 041 in rail blue and grey, September 1982.

Right: Departing Stratford Low Level is Class 313/1 three-car EMU No. 313 110 of Silverlink Metro on a North London line service to Richmond, 3 October 2007. The Class 313/1s had extra shoegear compared to the Class 313/0s to enable them to work the North London Richmond–Stratford and the Euston–Watford Jct. services.

Nearing Gospel Oak on a Stratford–Richmond North London line service is London Overground Class 313/1 three-car EMU No. 313 107 in London Overground-branded Silverlink livery, 21 February 2008.

Class 313/0 three-car EMU No. 313 029 of First Capital Connect approaching Welham Green on a Welwyn Garden City–Moorgate service, 12 May 2014.

Strathclyde PTE Class 313/0 inner suburban three-car EMU No. 314 202 in the PTE's 'retro' carmine and cream livery departing Glasgow Central on a Cathcart Circle service (Glasgow Central–Cathcart–Glasgow Central), 9 October 2007.

Ready to depart Glasgow Central on a Cathcart Circle service via Maxwell Park is Strathclyde PTE Class 314 three-car EMU No. 314 216, 9 October 2007. Note the First Group logo on the cab-front indicating the primary operator First Scotrail, who at that time ran the Glasgow suburban network on behalf of Strathclyde PTE.

Class 314 three-car EMU No. 314 203 of Scotrail in Saltire livery leaving Paisley (Gilmour Street) on a Gourock–Glasgow (Central) service, 1 July 2015.

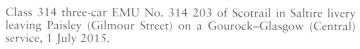

Descending Bethnal Green Bank on a Gidea Park–Liverpool Street service is BR (ER) inner suburban Class 315 four-car EMU No. 315 806 in rail blue and grey livery, September 1982.

Passing the Docklands Light Railway station at Pudding Mill Lane on a Shenfield–Liverpool Street service is ONE Class 315 four-car EMU No. 315 804, 3 October 2007. The set is in West Anglia Great Northern blue livery but with Great Eastern branding and yet no ONE branding!

Above left: Leaving Stratford is Class 315 four-car EMU No. 315 805 of National Express East Anglia in NXEA-branded ONE livery on a Liverpool Street–Shenfield service, 25 November 2008.

Above right: Approaching Forest Gate on a Liverpool Street–Shenfield service is Class 315 four-car EMU No. 315 821 of TfL Rail in their white livery with blue stripe and doors, 13 September 2015.

Above left: Arriving at Southport from Liverpool Central on a sunny day, November 1978, is the first of the BR (LMR) Class 507 inner suburban three-car EMUs, No. 507 001, in rail blue and grey livery, September 1982.

Above right: Calling at Birkenhead North on a New Brighton–Liverpool Central service is Merseyrail Class 507 three-car EMU, No. 507 021, in Merseyrail silver-grey and yellow livery on a very drizzly and dank 8 November 2010.

The forty-three sets of the class were built by BREL's York works in 1979–80 as a four-car version of the Class 507s. When the units were eventually transferred to Merseyside (to replace Class 503s) in 1981–84 following the introduction of the Class 455s built specifically for SR services, the Class 508/0 sets were reduced to three cars (and reclassified 508/1) to match the Class 507s. The TSOs were then inserted into Class 455/7s (built with just three cars) to make them up to four-car sets before entering service, the lower roof of the former Class 508 cars looking somewhat odd relative to the full height of the other Class 455 cars.

In 1996 Connex South East hired twelve sets, reclassified 508/2, for Kent services owing to a shortage of Class 466s, but from 2006 to 2008 the units were placed in store. In 2003 Silverlink leased three sets for working the Watford DC lines and these were altered to work with the Class 313s which operated most of these services, being reclassified 508/3. They have now been replaced with Class 378s. The Class 508/2s and 3s were scrapped in 2013, although one of the former remains in departmental use.

Departing Waterloo for Shepperton is BR (SR) Class 508/0 inner suburban four-car EMU No. 508 033 in rail blue and grey livery, September 1982.

Above left: Departing Euston on a Watford Jct. service is Class 508/3 three-car EMU No. 508 301 (ex-No. 508 102) of London Overground in LO-branded Silverlink Metro, 13 December 2007.

Above right: Class 508/2 three-car EMU No. 508 205 (originally No. 508 109) nearing East Croydon on a London Bridge–Tunbridge Wells service, 21 November 2008. This was during the last days of the Southeastern service to Tunbridge Wells before transfer to Southern, despite the unit having recently been repainted in Southeastern livery from the original Connex South East livery.

Right: In gentle drizzle, Merseyrail Class 508/1 three-car EMU No. 508 124 stops at Birkenhead North on a Liverpool Central–West Kirby service, 8 November 2010.

4

Later Second Generation EMUs – Standard BR Mark 3 Designs 1981–95

BREL (York) Standard Mark 3 750 V DC 3rd Rail/25 kV AC Overhead Outer Suburban Class 457/316 Three- and Four-car EMUs

In 1981 British Rail decided to build two DEMU prototypes of Class 210 (a three-car set and a four-car set) with the cars being based on the standard BR Mark 3 coach which employed fully integral construction. It was intended to be the basis of a new 'standard multiple unit' for production in DMU, DEMU and EMU (both AC and DC) versions. In the event, though successful, the DEMU proved too costly and wasteful of space (with the engine in the body) to put into production. However, it did form the basis for DMU and EMU classes.

Moreover, in the late 1980s BR wanted to test three-phase AC motors instead of the traditional DC variety for the proposed Networker design and the by then redundant Class 210s were chosen for conversion to a test bed. Consequently, in 1988–89 the driving trailers (converted to driving motors with 3rd rail DC equipment) from both sets plus two trailers were formed into a prototype four-car EMU (with all standard class accommodation) for trial on the Southern Region and classified 457, with the number (45)7001.

After a year's testing, it was then decided to transfer the set to the 25 kV AC overhead Clacton route on the Eastern Region. Consequently, a Class 313 trailer with pantograph equipment for the overhead lines replaced one of the Class 457 trailers and the four-car unit was reclassified 316 and numbered 316 999. The prototype proved successful in both forms, although it was taken out of service in 1991. Meanwhile, EMU versions of the Class 210 DEMU had already entered production in the form of Classes 317, 318, 319, 320, 321, 322, 455 and 456. Only car No. 67300 is preserved.

BREL (York and Derby) Standard Mark 3 25 kV AC Overhead Outer Suburban/Stansted Express Class 317 Four-car EMUs

The Class 317s were the first production EMUs to be based on the standard BR Mark 3 coach bodyshell as used in the Class 210 DEMU prototypes. Unlike the aluminium bodies of the previous 1972 design, the Mark 3 employed steel. Like the Class 210/316/457 standard MU, the Class 317s were gangwayed throughout. They were built by

Preserved in Network South East livery at the Electric Railway Museum, Coventry, on 10 September 2011 is a unique survivor, Driving Motor Second Open No. 67300 that originally formed part of prototype Class 457 four-car DC set No. 7001 and later part of Class 316 four-car AC set No. 316 999.

BREL in both York and Derby for 25 kV AC overhead lines. The forty-eight Class 317/1 sets were built in 1981–82 for the newly electrified 'BedPan' (Bedford–St Pancras/Moorgate) service, replacing the Class 127 DMUs.

On the formation of the new Thameslink route in 1986, the Class 317/1s were displaced by Class 319s and moved to the WCML Euston–Milton Keynes/Northampton services, replacing Class 310s. From 1989 they were again displaced by Class 321s and were transferred to work out of King's Cross and Liverpool Street. Many were hired out to work on the LT&S line out of Fenchurch Street during the years 1996–2002 (replacing Class 302s).

The twenty-four Class 317/2s were built in 1985–87 for Great Northern line services from King's Cross to Cambridge and Peterborough, replacing Class 312s, and later Great Eastern line services from Liverpool Street to Cambridge and King's Lynn; like the earlier 317/1s, the 317/2s had both first and standard class accommodation. The Class 317/2s had a modified front end (similar to the later batches of the Class 455s). In 1998–99 the sets were completely refurbished by Railcare, Wolverton, and reclassified 317/6. In 2000, nine Class 317/1s were extensively refurbished by Railcare and had new front ends fitted for working the Liverpool Street–Stansted Airport service, being reclassified 317/7. In 2005–06, twelve further 317/1s were refurbished by Wabtec, Doncaster, as Class 317/8 for the Stansted Airport service, but to a different specification from the 317/7s. An additional twenty-four Class 317/1s were refurbished in 2005 for West Anglia Metro services as Class 317/5.

BR (LMR) Class 317/1 outer-suburban four-car EMU No. 317 333 in rail blue and grey livery at St Pancras, having just arrived from Bedford, August 1984.

Above: Waiting to depart for St Pancras is BR (LMR) Class 317/1 four-car EMU No. 317 305 at Bedford, May 1984.

Right: ONE Stansted Express Class 317/7 four-car EMU No. 317 729 (originally No. 317 329), with revised light clusters, departs Bethnal Green on its way to Stansted Airport, 29 August 2007. At this time this unit was the last Class 317 in the ONE Stansted Express livery of metallic grey, black and orange, all the others being in the replacement metallic two-tone blue livery.

Above left: National Express East Anglia Class 317/5 four-car EMU No. 317 514 (originally No. 317 318) in de-branded ONE livery and yet to receive the NXEA white stripe and branding. The set is approaching Bethnal Green on a Bishop's Stortford–Liverpool service, 21 February 2008.

Above right: National Express East Anglia Class 317/8 four-car EMU No. 317 888 (originally No. 317 331) in a later version of the Stansted Express livery but with the NXEA white stripe and branding. The set is seen at Stratford on an ECS working, 29 August 2008.

Above left: National Express East Anglia's Class 317/6 four-car EMU No. 317 649 (originally No. 317 249) on an ECS working at Stratford, March 2010. Remarkably for this time, No. 317 649 is still in original West Anglia Great Northern livery of white with grey swish and blue and orange stripes, but with NXEA branding; it was probably the last unit in this livery on 3 March 2010. The 317/6s were converted from 317/2s by Railcare, Wolverton, in 1998–99 for Great Eastern lines out of Liverpool Street. The 317/2s and 317/6s differed from the 317/1s by having the warning horns relocated from above the cab to coupling level and no box above the cab gangway.

Above right: Nearing Alexandra Palace is First Capital Connect's Class 317/1 four-car EMU No. 317 345 *Driver John Webb* on a King's Cross–Cambridge service, 12 May 2014.

BREL (York) Standard Mark 3 25 kV AC Overhead Outer Suburban Class 318 Three-car EMUs

The Class 318s were built by BREL (York) in 1985–87 with all standard-class accommodation for outer suburban work on Glasgow's 25 kV AC network. The Class 318s, effectively a three-car version of the Class 317s, were built with a central gangway in the cab front. However, on refurbishment by Hunslet-Barclay in 2005–07, the gangway was removed and plated over to improve the driver's accommodation.

BREL (York) Standard Mark 3 25 kV AC Overhead/750 V DC 3rd Rail Outer Suburban Class 319 Four-car EMUs

The Class 319s are dual voltage AC/DC sets, built by BREL (York) for cross-London Thameslink services between Bedford and Brighton with first-class and standard-class accommodation. Because the Class 319s used the reopened Snow Hill tunnel through London, the body profile of the Class 319s differed from the earlier Class 317s, as did the cab, which had a sloping front incorporating a central door for evacuation purposes in the tunnel instead of the gangway of the Class 317s. Except for emergency purposes, the ability for communication between sets was thus dispensed with. They were the first BR EMUs to use thyristor control instead of camshafts.

The first batch of sixty Class 319/0s was built in 1987–88, followed in 1990 by twenty-six Class 319/1s, with minor differences, for expanded Thameslink services. Both subclasses have subsequently been refurbished. Seven Class 319/0s were refurbished by Railcare, Wolverton, in the late 1990s as Class 319/2s for Connex South Central's Victoria/London Bridge–Brighton services, although they were later transferred back to Thameslink. The Class 319/3s were converted from all twenty-six Class 319/1s by Eastleigh in 1997–99 for the Thameslink City Metro service (Luton–Sutton/Wimbledon) and lost their first class accommodation. In contrast, forty Class 319/0s were refurbished as Class 319/4s for the Thameslink City Flyer service (Bedford–Brighton), leaving just thirteen Class 317/0s still so classified. In 2015, twenty Class 319/3s were transferred to Northern to operate recently electrified lines in the north-west, the 750 V DC equipment being removed. Two Class 319/4s have also been transferred to work the Watford Jct.–St Albans City Abbey Flyer service.

BREL (York) Standard Mk.3 25 kV AC Overhead Outer Suburban Class 320 Three-car EMUs

The Class 320s were ordered specifically for the Glasgow 25 kV AC outer suburban North Clyde and Argyll lines and had all standard-class seating. Twenty-two were built by BREL (York) in 1990 to replace Class 303s and 311s. They were effectively a three-car version of the Class 321s with a similarly revised cab-front with no door or gangway. The sets had all standard class accommodation.

BREL (York) Standard Mk.3 25 kV AC Overhead Outer Suburban Class 321 Four-car EMUs

The Class 321s adopted a revised cab design to the previous standard flat-fronted, gangwayed cab of the Class 317s and 318s and were a variation of the more attractive sloping front of the Class 319s, but without the central emergency door and with a two-paned windscreen.

Approaching Dalmuir on a Balloch–Airdrie via Singer service is ScotRail Class 318 three-car EMU No. 318 266 *Strathclyder* still in Stratchclyde PTE carmine and cream livery, 1 July 2015.

Class 318 three-car EMU No. 318 265 of ScotRail in Strathclyde PTE livery leaving Whifflet on a Milngavie–Carmyle–Motherwell service, 2 July 2015.

At Blackfriars on a Luton–Sutton–Wimbledon service is First Capital Connect Class 319/3 outer suburban four-car EMU No. 319 373 in FCC-branded revised Thameslink silver and blue livery, 28 November 2007.

Above left: Emerging out of Snow Hill Tunnel on the approach to Farringdon is First Capital Connect Class 319/3 four-car EMU No. 319 380 in FCC livery on a service to St Albans City, 25 February 2008. The line to the left is to Moorgate, which closed in March 2009.

Above right: First Capital Connect Class 319/4 four-car EMU No. 319 436 is passing through Sydenham on a Brighton–Luton service, 12 June 2009.

Right: Framed by what passes for an impressive signal gantry in these days of colour light signals, Class 319/4 four-car EMU No. 319 443 of First Capital Connect is on a Sutton–Bedford service at East Hyde, 15 April 2014.

With the rolling fields of Bedfordshire as a backdrop, First Capital Connect's Class 319/3 four-car EMU No. 319 366 passes East Hyde on a Sutton-bound service, 15 April 2014.

Once of Southern but now of First Capital Connect, Class 319/0 four-car EMU No. 319 012 *Cheriton*, still in Southern livery but with FCC branding, passes Thrales End, north of Wheathampstead, on a Brighton–Bedford service, 15 April 2014. The unit is coupled to a sister set in full FCC livery.

First Capital Connect's Class 319/4 four-car EMU No. 319 452 glides past Thrales End on a Bedford service, 15 April 2014.

At St Albans on a Bedford–Gatwick Airport service is First Capital Connect's Class 319/2 four-car EMU No. 319 219 in FCC branded Southern livery, 15 April 2014.

Class 319/3 four-car EMU No. 319 382 of Northern (with Northern Electrics branding) crossing Mill Lane Viaduct over Newton Brook near Newton-le-Willows station on a Manchester (Piccadilly)–Liverpool (Lime Street) service, 13 August 2015.

Seen approaching Whifflet on a Dalmuir–Motherwell–Cumbernauld service is Class 320 outer suburban three-car EMU No. 320 306 of ScotRail in 'Saltire' livery, 2 July 2015.

BREL (York) built the Class 321s: sixty-six Class 321/3 sets in 1988–90 for GEML services out of Liverpool Street and LT&S services out of Fenchurch Street (replacing Classes 305, 308, 309, 310 and 312); forty-eight Class 321/4 sets in 1989–90 for WCML services between Euston and Birmingham (eleven sets were later reallocated to the GEML and thirteen to the GN), and three Class 321/9s in 1991 for the West Yorkshire PTE's Leeds–Doncaster line. The Class 321/3 and 4s have two-class accommodation but the 321/9s have standard-class only. There have been several reallocations for the 321/3s and 321/4s and seven of the latter, reduced to three-car sets (and possibly reclassified 320/2), will go to ScotRail.

Departing Birmingham New Street on a Euston service is Silverlink County Class 321/4 outer suburban four-car EMU No. 321 414, 21 September 2007.

Leaving Leeds for Doncaster via Wakefield Westgate is West Yorkshire PTE Class 321/9 four-car EMU No. 321 903 in combined West Yorkshire PTE/ Northern Rail livery, 30 April 2008.

Approaching Watford Jct. bound for Euston is London Midland Class 321/4 four-car EMU No. 321 430 in de-branded Silverlink livery, 2 July 2008.

Class 321/3 four-car EMU No. 321 331 in National Express East Anglia-branded Great Eastern livery approaches Stratford, 19 November 2008.

Recently transferred from Silverlink and newly repainted into London Midland livery is Class 321/4 four-car EMU No. 321 411 pulling into Watford Jct. on a Birmingham New Street–Euston service, 25 June 2009.

Above left: Approaching Stratford at speed on a Clacton–Liverpool St service is Class 321/4 four-car EMU No. 321 448 in National Express East Anglia-branded Great Eastern livery, 25 June 2009.

Above right: Seen at Stratford on an ECS working is a National Express East Anglia Class 319/3 four-car EMU No. 321 308 in NXEA livery, 6 April 2010.

Above left: First Capital Connect's Class 321/4 four-car EMU No. 321 410 passing Harringay station on a King's Cross–Peterborough service, 12 May 2014.

Above right: Approaching Harringay from King's Cross is First Capital Connect's snappily named Class 321/4 four-car EMU No. 321 409 *Dame Alice Owen's School 400 Years of Learning*, 12 May 2014.

BREL (York) Standard Mark 3 25 kV AC Overhead Stansted Express/Outer Suburban Class 322 Four-car EMUs

BREL's York plant built five Class 322 sets in 1990 as a version of the Class 321s specifically for the Liverpool Street–Stansted Airport service, but from 1997 they were replaced on this service with other classes and have been transferred to several other operators, including ScotRail (where they were reduced to all standard class) and currently Northern, operating mainly on Leeds–Doncaster services.

ABB (Derby) Standard Mark 3 25 kV AC Overhead/750 V DC 3rd Rail Postal Class 325 Four-car EMUs

ABB built sixteen dual-voltage Class 325s in 1995, adapted from the Class 319 design, specifically for postal use by Royal Mail between London and Glasgow/Edinburgh (and later Newcastle). The sets were fitted with the then new ABB Networker cab. They had no gangways. They were the last MU to be based on the Mark 3 bodyshell and the last parcels stock built in the days of British Rail.

Left: First Scot Rail Class 322 four-car EMU No. 322 483 leaves Edinburgh Waverley for North Berwick, 6 May 2010.

Opposite: At speed passing Headstone Lane is Royal Mail Class 325 four-car postal EMU No. 325 002 on a Willesden Railnet–Shieldmuir mail service, 14 October 2009.

BREL (Derby) Standard Mark 3 750 V DC 3rd Rail Class 442 (5-WES) Wessex Express Five-car EMUs

The twenty Class 442s – or 5-WES in the old Southern Region classification – were built in 1988–89 and were based on the BR Mark 3 coach design. They had a high standard of accommodation, with first and standard class and a buffet car. They were built specifically for the Waterloo–Bournemouth–Weymouth service following the belated extension of the 750 V DC 3rd rail electrification to the latter town, the 442s replacing 4-REPs and 4-TCs. Later, they were also used on Waterloo–Southampton–Portsmouth services.

Following privatisation, South West Trains decided they cost too much to run and they were placed in store in early 2007, SWT replacing them with Class 444 and 450 Desiros. However, the following year Southern found itself short of trains and restored them to service, gradually renovating them extensively, removing the buffet in the process. They were then put to use on the Gatwick Express and Victoria–Brighton services, controversially replacing purpose-built Class 460 Junipers on the former service. Although they had many teething troubles on introduction, they subsequently became very reliable. The world speed record for DC 3rd rail is held by No. (44)2401 at 108mph, achieved in 1988.

BR Class 442 (SR Class 5-WES) Wessex Express five-car EMU No. (44)2409 (formerly named *Bournemouth Orchestras*) in Network South East livery and with the original four digit unit number at Weymouth on a service to Waterloo, August 1991. The NSE livery seems to me to have suited the Class 442s particularly well.

Above left: Non-refurbished Class 442 five-car EMU No. (44)2418 (formerly named *Wessex Cancer Trust*) of Southern but still in South West Trains livery and still with the original four-digit unit number. It is pictured passing Streatham Common on a Victoria–Gatwick Airport service, 23 June 2009.

Above right: Class 442 five-car EMU No. 442 414 of Southern in Gatwick Express livery on a Victoria–Gatwick Airport service passing Battersea Park, 1 July 2010.

BREL (York) Standard Mark 3 750 V DC 3rd Rail Inner Suburban Class 455 (originally Class 510) Four-car EMUs

The Class 455s, which employ the same bodyshell as the Class 317s, were for inner suburban services on BR Southern Region's 750 V DC network and had all standard class accommodation. They were gangwayed throughout when built. Ordered as Class 510, they were reclassified 455 before entering service. BREL (York) built several batches with a confusing classification system.

The first series was built in 1982–84, consisting of seventy-four Class 455/8s for Waterloo services (twenty-eight later operated by South West Trains) and Victoria and London Bridge services (forty-six later operated by Southern, which plated over the front gangway to enable cab air conditioning to be fitted). The second series of 1984–85 were the forty-three Class 455/7s for Waterloo services (later South West Trains) which had a revised front end with air horns relocated from the roof to coupler level and revised lamp clusters. Interestingly, the Class 455/7s were built as three-car sets but each had added a TSO taken from the Class 508s, these having a lower roof than standard. The third series of 1985 were the twenty Class 455/9s, now operated by South West Trains, similar to the 455/7s but with all new-build cars. For some reason, the Class 455s never had an (unofficial) SR-style classification even though later classes, such as the Juniper and Desiro types did.

Opposite above: Just arrived at Waterloo from Weybridge is BR (SR) Class 455/8 inner suburban four-car EMU No. (45)5801, March 1984. The set, the very first Class 455 built as one of the first series of Class 455s, is in rail blue and grey livery. This series of Class 455s had air horns and a box above the cabs' central gangway.

Opposite below: Seen at Clapham Jct. on a Kingston–Waterloo service is South West Trains Class 455/9 four-car EMU No. (45)5913, 23 July 2007. The set, one of the third series of Class 455s, is in SWT's inner suburban livery. This series, and the earlier second, had a revised front end from the first series, having the air horns moved from the roof to coupler level and revised lamp clusters.

Southern Class 455/8 (first series) four-car EMU No. 455 811 is seen approaching the now demolished train shed at London Bridge, 11 December 2008. Note the front gangway has been removed and plated-up to enable cab air conditioning to be fitted.

Stopping at Sutton, Southern Class 455/8 (first series) four-car EMU No. 455 837 is on an Epsom–Victoria service, 24 March 2009.

Seen at the rather higgledy-piggledy Effingham Jct. station, South West Trains Class 455/7 (second series) four-car EMU No. (45)5727 in SWT's inner suburban livery is on a Guildford–Epsom–Waterloo service, 24 March 2009.

Class 455/8 (first series) four-car EMU No. 455 832 of Southern at Norwood Jct., 12 September 2015.

BREL (York) Standard Mark 3 750 V DC 3rd Rail Inner Suburban Class 456 Two-car EMUs

Constructed in 1990–91 by BREL's York works, the twenty-four Class 456 two-car 750 V DC 3rd rail sets were replacements for Class 416 2-EPBs on the Central Division of BR's Network South East.

In 2014 they were transferred from Southern to South West Trains. Their accommodation is all standard class and they have gangways within each set. Their cab-front is similar to the Class 320/321/322 EMUs, although with cabling at a higher level. The Class 456 was the last passenger MU design to be based on the Mark 3 body design.

Above left: Coming to a stop at Whyteleaf South on a London Bridge–Caterham service is Southern Class 456 two-car EMU No. 456 004, 11 December 2008.

Above right: Approaching London Bridge on a service from Epsom Downs is Southern Class 456 two-car EMU No. 456 015 coupled to sister units, 21 November 2008.

Opposite: Nearing Battersea Park on a South London line service from Victoria to London Bridge is inner suburban Class 456 two-car EMU No. 456 006 of Southern in Transport for London promotional livery, 23 July 2007.

5

Third Generation EMUs – Designs Towards and Under Privatisation: BREL/ABB Networker Family 1991–95

ABB (York) 25 kV AC Overhead/750 V DC 3rd Rail Class 365 Networker Express Four-car EMUs

The forty-one Class 365 four-car EMUs were built by ABB at York in 1994–95 and were the last trains built there before its closure. With the cancellation of the Universal Networker dual-voltage, express design (proposed Classes 371 and 381) by BR because of a lack of funding, BR decided to procure a cheaper, two-class, longer-distance, express version of their suburban Class 465 – effectively an EMU version of ABB's Networker Express DMU which in turn was a development of BREL's Networker Turbo DMU. Like all Networker EMU classes, the Class 365s are gangwayed only within each set.

The Class 365s were built with dual-voltage capability, although the sixteen used on Network South East lines south of the Thames (London–Kent) were completed with 750 V DC 3rd rail equipment only whilst the remaining twenty-five for NSE lines north of the Thames (King's Cross–Peterborough and Cambridge/King's Lynn) had 25 kV AC overhead equipment. However, when in 2004 all units were allocated to the latter service, then operated by West Anglia Great Northern, the DC equipment on the first batch was replaced with 25 kV AC equipment.

As built, the Class 365s looked identical to the Class 465s but on refurbishment by Bombardier, Doncaster, in 2006–07 and concentration on GN lines, a new grill on the cab front gave them a 'smiley face' visage! When the electrification of the Great Western Thames Valley Line is completed, it is planned that twenty-one sets will be transferred to FGW.

BREL and ABB (York)/Metro-Cammell (Washwood Heath) 750 V DC 3rd Rail Inner and Outer Suburban Class 465 Networker Four-car EMUs

The 750 V DC 3rd rail four-car Class 465s were the first of what British Rail intended to be their next generation of standard AC and DC EMUs, the Networker, of which there was to be a DMU version also (the Networker Turbo and Networker Express). The Networker EMU design was to be produced in inner suburban, outer suburban and express forms.

The 465s were for Network South East inner suburban services to replace Class 415 4-EPBs on Victoria/Charing Cross/Cannon Street/

First Capital Connect's express Class 365 four-car EMU No. 365 519 *Peterborough: Environment Capital* in associated promotional livery on a Peterborough service speeds past Hornsey, 12 May 2014.

Above left: Slowing for its Potter's Bar stop is First Capital Connect's Class 365 four-car EMU No. 365 509 on a Peterborough–King's Cross service, 12 May 2014.

Above right: At speed near Broxbourne Park is Class 365 four-car EMU No. 365 509 of First Capital Connect on a King's Cross–Peterborough service, 12 May 2014.

Left: Passing Harringay station is Class 365 four-car EMU No. 365 525 of First Capital Connect recently repainted but not in the standard FCC 'urban lights' livery but in the new Thameslink light grey livery on a King's Cross service, 12 May 2014.

Above left: BREL-built inner suburban Class 465/0 four-car EMU No. 465 041 of Southeastern (but still in BR Network South East blue, white and grey livery) calls at Eynsford on a Victoria–Ashford service, June 2005.

Above right: Charing Cross-bound inner suburban ABB-built Class 465/1 four-car EMU No. 465 167 of Southeastern is seen passing a sister unit travelling in the opposite direction at London Bridge, 4 October 2007. The set is in Southeatern's white, yellow, black and grey livery, which was actually a revised livery introduced by Connex Southeastern before it lost its franchise, but in the event became more associated with the successor operator GoVia's Southeastern.

Right: Departing Victoria is Metro-Cammell-built inner suburban Class 465/2 four-car EMU No. 465 242 of Southeastern, 5 June 2008.

GEC-Alsthom (Washwood Heath) 750 V DC 3rd Rail Inner Suburban Class 466 Networker Two-car EMUs

The Class 466 was simply a two-car version of the Class 465 and intended for similar inner suburban duties on BR Network South East lines from London into Kent, replacing Class 416 2-EPBs. GEC-Alsthom built forty-three sets at the former Metro-Cammell Washwood Heath works in 1993–94.

Blackfriars/London Bridge–Kent services. They were originally called Kent Link Networker. Fifty Class 465/0 sets were built in 1991–93 at the York works when it was still under BREL management; they have high-density, standard-class seating only, as have the forty-seven Class 465/1s built in 1993–94 by what was then ABB at York, and the fifty Class 465/2s by Metro-Cammell's Washwood Heath works in 1991–93.

In 2005, thirty-four Class 465/2s were extensively refurbished, with first-class seating replacing some standard-class seating to take over from ageing 4-VEPs on outer suburban services in Kent and reclassified 465/9. In 1992, one Class 465/0 was temporarily modified as a Class 465/3 to be the prototype of the Class 365.

Top left: Pulling into Chatham is Metro-Cammell-built outer suburban Class 465/9 four-car EMU No. 465 902 (formerly No. 465 202) of Southeastern, 12 June 2008.

Opposite above: Approaching the South Eastern side of Victoria station is GEC-Alsthom-built inner suburban Class 466 two-car EMU No. 466 002 of Southeastern, 5 June 2008.

Opposite below: Leaving London Bridge is Southeastern Class 466 two-car EMU No. 466 008, 1 July 2010.

6

Third Generation EMUs – Designs Towards and Under Privatisation: Hunslet Transportation Projects 1992–93

Hunslet Transportation Projects 25 kV AC Overhead Inner Suburban Class 323 Three-car EMUs

Hunslet Transportation Projects built forty-three Class 323 three-car sets at their Hunslet, Leeds works in 1992–93 for BR Regional Railways' 25 kV AC inner suburban lines in Birmingham (twenty-six sets) and Manchester (seventeen sets). The accommodation of the Class 323 is high-density, standard-class only and the EMUs are gangwayed just within each set.

Historically, the class was significant on several counts. The sets were the first privately built, newly designed EMUs ordered by BR since nationalisation and were the first EMU design ordered by BR in the 1990s. Also, they were some of the last EMUs built pre-privatisation; however, so protracted was their introduction – with the sets having to go into long-term storage whilst many teething problems were sorted out – that it was not until 1996 that the sets entered full service, after privatisation had begun in 1994. Moreover, they were the last trains built by Hunslet before it ceased operation, another mark of an end of an era.

The serious reliability problems which accompanied their initial entry into service with West Midlands PTE (as Centro) on the newly electrified Cross City line in Birmingham resulted in the first generation DMUs they were supposed to replace soldiering on until 1995, until the reliability of the 323s finally became acceptable. In the north-west, the Class 323s, operated by Manchester PTE, replaced Class 304 and 305 EMUs and their reliability here was also very poor to begin with, although considerable efforts to improve matters were eventually successful and they now have a good reliability record.

About to depart Manchester Piccadilly for Alderley Edge is Northern's Class 323 inner suburban three-car EMU No. 323 233, 20 September 2007.

Leaving Birmingham New Street is Central Trains Class 323 three-car EMU No. 323 202 in Centro livery of light grey and green with a blue stripe, 21 September 2007.

Departing Birmingham New Street is Class 323 three-car EMU No. 323 208 of London Midland in LM's then-new livery, 19 May 2008.

Third Generation EMUs – Designs under Privatisation: CAF/Siemens Family 1997–98

CAF (Zaragoza)/Siemens (Verdingen–Krefeld) 25 kV AC Overhead Heathrow Express Class 332 Three-, Four- and Five-car EMUs

The fourteen Class 332s were built in 1997–98 as three-car units but were first strengthened to four-car sets and then to five-car sets with new cars built in 2002. The bodies were constructed by CAF in Zaragoza and fitted out in Siemens' Verdingen works, Krefeld. They were specifically designed for the new 25 kV AC Heathrow Express service and have a particularly high standard of two-class accommodation. They are gangwayed within sets.

CAF (Zaragoza)/Siemens (Verdingen–Krefeld) 25 kV AC Overhead West Yorkshire Outer Suburban Class 333 Three- and Four-car EMUs

The sixteen Class 333 sets are based on the Heathrow Express Class 332s, although have high-density single-class accommodation, more suitable for the West Yorkshire PTE's 25 kV AC services (Leeds/ Bradford Foster Square–Skipton/Ilkley). They replaced Class 308s. The 333s were, like the 332s, built by CAF and Siemens in 2001 as three-car sets and strengthened to four cars in 2002–03. The sets have internal gangways only.

Speeding through Hayes and Harlington are two Heathrow Express Class 332 three-car EMUs of which the leading unit appears to be only of three cars at a time when all sets were supposed to have been increased to four or five cars. Unfortunately, it is not clear what number the three-car set is; it may (appropriately) be No. 332 003. It is in RBS promotional livery, 7 April 2009.

With its first-class end near to the buffers, Class 332 five-car EMU No. 332 009 in Heathrow Express livery and with RBS promotional branding is about to depart Paddington for Heathrow Airport, 24 July 2008.

Under Brunel's superb train shed at Paddington is Heathrow Express Class 332 four-car EMU No. 332 013 in Vodafone advertising livery, 12 June 2014.

About to depart Leeds for Ilkley is Class 333 four-car EMU No. 333 010 in original West Yorkshire PTE/Northern Spirit livery but with Metrotrain/Northern Rail branding, 30 April 2008.

Third Generation EMUs – Designs under Privatisation: Alstom Juniper Family 1998–2002

Alstom (Washwood Heath) 25 kV AC Overhead Outer Suburban Class 334 Juniper Three-car EMUs

This class was a member of Alstom's Juniper range and was built at Washwood Heath in the years 1999–2002 for Glasgow's 25 kV AC outer suburban services. The sets have medium-density, standard-class seating. They have full-width cabs without gangway connections but have gangways within the sets. The Class 334s had a lengthy introduction into service because of numerous technical problems with the result that the PTE only paid for thirty-eight of the forty sets delivered! They replaced the Class 303 and 311 Blue Trains.

Alstom (Washwood Heath) 750 V DC 3rd Rail Outer Suburban Class 458 Juniper (or 4-JOP and 5-JOP) Four- and Five-car EMUs

Thirty Class 458 (or 4-JOP) four-car EMUs were built at Alstom's Saltley plant in 1998–2002, the first of the Juniper family for a British TOC–South West Trains. SWT wanted them for their 750 V DC 3rd rail outer suburban services from Waterloo, replacing ageing 4-CEPs and 4-VEPs. Unlike their sister Class 334s in Scotland, the 458s had gangway connections in the cab-end – much to the aesthetic disadvantage of the Class 458s! However, like the Class 344s, the Class 458s were plagued with technical problems and their reliability was far worse than the slam-door stock they replaced. So poor was their availability that they were largely displaced from service in favour of Desiros in 2005–06. However, in the event the entire fleet was refurbished by Bournemouth depot in 2008–10 and returned to service on the Waterloo–Reading/Ascot/Guildford lines. So effective was the refurbishment that by 2010 the Class 458 became the most reliable EMU design on British railways.

Although the Class 458s had settled down to give good service, it was then decided – rather unexpectedly – to combine the four-car 458s with the eight-car 460s to form five-car 458/5s (or 5-JOPs), the first-class accommodation being replaced with standard class and standing room increased in the process. Improved cab gangways were also fitted. This process was carried out by Wabtec, Doncaster and Brush, Loughborough, in 2013–15. They were then switched to Waterloo–Eton Riverside, Windsor and Weybridge services.

Departing Glasgow Central, outer suburban Class 334 Juniper three-car DMU No. 334 040 of Strathclyde PTE heads for Wemyss Bay, 9 October 2007. The Class 334s were delivered with a variation on the Strathclyde PTE carmine and cream livery by the addition of a turquoise stripe.

Strathclyde PTE Class 334 three-car DMU No. 334 030 approaching Glasgow Central, 9 October 2007.

Departing Whifflet on a Cumbernauld–Motherwell–Glasgow Central service is Class 334 three-car DMU No. 334 023 of ScotRail in Saltire livery, 2 July 2015.

Seen at Staines on 24 March 2009 is Class 458/0 (or 4-JOP) Juniper express four-car EMU No. (45)8011 of South West Trains in the express/long-distance version of its livery, even though the Waterloo–Reading service on which the Class 458/0s were used is really an outer suburban one.

Class 458/5 (or 5-JOP) outer suburban five-car EMU No. 458 526 of South West Trains leaves Waterloo on a Windsor service, 13 August 2015. The livery of the lengthened Class 458s is the more appropriate SWT outer suburban livery than the express variety which they had as four-car sets – except that the revised sets now seem to be used on inner suburban services! In addition, the revised sets' numbering abandons the SWT practice of displaying only the last four figures of the set number and instead shows all six digits of the TOPS number.

Alstom (Washwood Heath) 750 V DC 3rd Rail Gatwick Express Class 460 (or 8-GAT) Juniper Eight-car EMUs

Built at the same time as the Class 458s at Alstom's Washwood Heath facility (1999–2001), the eight Class 460s (or 8-GAT) eight-car EMUs were specifically built for the Gatwick Express running between Victoria and Gatwick Airport; they replaced the Class 73/2 locomotives and Class 489 BR Mark 2 coach sets. The Class 460s had one driving car that (apart from the cab) was entirely given over to luggage. They were gangwayed only within each set and their streamlined cabs resulted in the 460s acquiring the nickname of Darth Vaders. In my opinion the design was the most spectacular and attractive of any British non-high-speed EMU.

In 2008, National Express lost the Gatwick Express franchise to Southern, who decided to replace the 460s with refurbished Class 442s, which took place in 2010–12. The sets were then disbanded and in 2013–15 most of their cars, suitably modified, were used to lengthen the Class 458s, four of the driving luggage cars then unfortunately becoming redundant in the process. With the streamlined cabs of the other reused driving cars being replaced with conventional cabs with gangway connections, the striking Darth Vaders will no longer be seen in service.

Gatwick Express Class 460 (or 8-GAT) Juniper eight-car EMU No. (460 0)02 at Clapham Jct. on a Gatwick Airport–Victoria service, 20 June 2008.

Above left: Class 460 (or 8-GAT) eight-car EMU No. (460 0)06 of Gatwick Express speeds through Clapham Jct. on a Gatwick Airport–Victoria service, 20 June 2008. By this time the Gatwick Express franchise had been absorbed by Southern but the Class 460s retained their Gatwick Express livery and largely remained dedicated to the Gatwick Airport route.

Above right: Class 460 (or 8-GAT) eight-car EMU No. (460 0)03 of Gatwick Express/Southern in Emirates (China) livery passing through Streatham Common on a Gatwick Airport–Victoria service, 25 June 2009.

Third Generation EMUs – Designs under Privatisation: Adtranz/Bombardier Electrostar Family 1999 and Continuing

Adtranz/Bombardier (Derby) 25 kV AC Overhead Outer Suburban Class 357 Electrostar Four-car EMUs

The Class 357s were the first of the Electrostar family which was a modular design based on the Adtranz/Bombardier Turbostar DMU design, sharing a common design platform; the Turbostars were in turn a development of BREL/ABB's Networker EMU/Network Turbo DMU. It is interesting to compare Adtranz/Bombardier's Electrostar development of BREL's Network Turbo concept with ABB/Metro-Cammell/GEC-Alsthom's Networker development of the same design. The Class 357s are gangwayed within each set but have a full-width cab.

The 25 kV AC Class 357s were built specifically for the London, Tilbury and Southend services from Fenchurch Street; although split into two subclasses, the two are identical – the designations simply reflecting different ownership. The forty-four Class 357/0s were built by Adtranz, Derby, in 1999–2001 to replace Class 310s and the twenty-eight Class 357/2s (what happened to Class 357/1?) were also built there by Bombardier (who had taken over Adtranz) in 2001–02 to replace Class 312s.

Considerable teething problems followed the Class 357s introduction, to such an extent that Adtranz supplied two extra 357/0s free of charge! But when the difficulties were resolved, the 357s settled down to perform reliably and efficiently, becoming the most reliable EMU in the UK in 2005–07. Coupled with their modern and comfortable interior, the 357s were a welcome change for the long-suffering commuters of the 'Misery Line' – as the LT&S route had been known.

Adtranz/Bombardier (Derby) 750 V DC 3rd Rail Outer Suburban/Express Class 375 Electrostar Three- and Four-car EMUs

The Class 375s were the second Electrostar design to be ordered, this time for the South Eastern franchise to replace BR Mark 1 slam-door stock on express (375/3-8 replacing 4-CEPs and 4-CIGs) or outer suburban services (375/9 replacing 4-VEPs) working out of Victoria, Charing Cross and Cannon Street to Kent and East Sussex. All are gangwayed throughout (unlike the previous Class 357s) and are four-car sets, except the 375/3s which have just three cars. All have two-class,

Above left: C2C Electrostar Class 357/2 outer suburban four-car EMU No. 357 204 *Derek Fowers* approaches Stratford at speed, 19 November 2008.

Above right: About to depart Braintree for Fenchurch Street is C2C Class 357/0 four-car EMU No. 357 018, 29 March 2010.

Right: Departing Limehouse on a Liverpool Street–Shoeburyness service is C2C Class 357/0 four-car EMU No. 357 032 in National Express white livery, 15 March 2010.

low-density accommodation, except the 375/9s, which have standard-class, high-density accommodation.

The first batch delivered by Adtranz, Derby, in 1999–2001 was thirty dual-voltage 375/6s (25 kV AC overhead and 750 V DC 3rd rail), whereas all subsequent subclasses simply had provision for 25 kV AC equipment but were fitted only for 750 V DC operation. Ten 375/3s and fifteen 375/7s followed in 2001–02, Adtranz by now having been taken over by Bombardier. The last batches built were the twenty-seven 357/9s in 2003–04 and thirty 375/8s in 2004.

Above: With the London Eye in the background, Southeastern express Class 375/8 four-car EMU No. 375 825 is at Waterloo East, 7 August 2007. When GoVia took over the Southeastern franchise from Connex they continued to use the latter's revised livery of white, grey, black and yellow.

Left: Southeastern Class 375/8 four-car EMU No. 375 816 nears London Bridge, 7 August 2007.

Above left: Departing the south-eastern platforms of Victoria is Southeastern express Class 375/3 three-car EMU No. 375 305, 5 June 2008.

Above right: Emerging out of the tunnel into Chatham station is Southeastern Class 375/3 three-car EMU No. 375 305, 7 August 2008.

Right: Departing London Bridge is outer suburban Class 375/9 four-car EMU No. 375 907 of Southeastern, 6 June 2010.

Bombardier (Derby) 750 V DC 3rd Rail Inner Suburban Class 376 Electrostar Five-car EMUs

The thirty-six Class 376s were built at Derby by Bombardier in 2004–05. They were a very high-density version of the Electrostar design, at first called Electrostar Metro, with no cab gangways, no toilets and tram-like accommodation (all standard class) for short-distance inner suburban services. The Class 376s were configured for 750 V DC 3rd rail services in the South East (Charing Cross and Canon Street to Kent) but had provision for 25 kV AC overhead equipment if ever needed. That need has not arisen so far!

Above: Class 376 inner suburban five-car EMU No. 376 016 of Southeastern calls at London Bridge's south-eastern platforms, 7 August 2007.

Left: Departing New Cross is Class 376 five-car EMU No. 376 028 of Southeastern, 6 June 2010.

Bombardier (Derby) 25 kV AC Overhead/750 V DC 3rd Rail Outer Suburban/Express Class 377 Electrostar Three-, Four- and Five-car EMUs

The Class 377s were ordered soon after the Class 375s for the neighbouring South Central franchise and were essentially the same design (apart from small differences); indeed, the first batches were initially classified 375s. Like the 375s, the 377s were intended for similar express and outer suburban services and replaced the same classes of slam-door EMUs on the Victoria/London Bridge–Brighton/South Coast/Southampton routes. All were built for express services with two-class accommodation, except the outer suburban 377/6s which had standard class only.

The Class 377s were built at Derby by Bombardier: sixty-four four-car 377/1s in 2002–03; fifteen four-car 377/2s in 2003–04; twenty-eight three-car 377/3s in 2001–02; seventy-five four-car 377/4s in 2004–05; twenty-three four-car 377/5s in 2008–09; twenty-six five-car 377/6s in 2012–13 and eight five-car 377/7s in 2013–14, making a grand total of 239 units.

Although the entire class was built for Southern, some 377/2s and, from delivery, every 377/5 were subleased to First Capital Connect for Thameslink services as a stop-gap until the delivery of the Class 385s – which in turn were a stop gap for the Siemens Class 700s! The 377s were designed for dual voltage and all were fitted for 750 V DC 3rd rail operation but the only subclasses fitted with 25 kV AC overhead equipment were the 377/2s (for Milton Keynes–Watford Jct.–South Croydon services) and the 377/5s (for Thameslink). The 377/6 and 7s employed the slightly modified bodyshell of the Class 379s.

The first sets to enter service were the Class 377/3s (then classified 375/3s) but only after considerable delays because of a major upgrade which had to be carried out to the 750 V DC network to cope with the increased electrical demands of the new sets compared to their predecessors.

Bombardier (Derby) 25 kV AC Overhead/750 V DC 3rd Rail Inner Suburban Class 378 Capitalstar Three-, Four- and Five-car EMUs

With Transport for London taking over the former Silverlink services in London in 2006, and with plans to upgrade and extend the East London line, TfL decided to order a very high density, standard class only, version of the Electrostar which was dubbed Capitalstar. The 378s were based on the Class 376s though with emergency doors in the cab-ends and a tube-style interior.

The first order for twenty-four three-car 378/0s was built in 2008 by Bombardier at Derby as dual voltage units for the North London and West London Lines and the Euston–Watford Jct. service. A fourth car was added to the Class 378/0s in 2010, when they were reclassified 378/2. A follow-on order resulted in thirteen more 378/2s being built in 2011 as four-car sets from the outset. A further order was for twenty four-car 378/1s which were built in 2009–10 for the 750 V DC East London and South London lines, although they had provision to be retro-fitted with 25 kV AC equipment. In 2014–15 all sets from both subclasses were strengthened again with a fifth car to cater for the huge increase in passenger numbers experienced on TfL's services.

Above left: Seen at Clapham Jct. is Brighton-bound Southern express Class 377/1 four-car EMU No. 377 130, 20 June 2008.

Above right: Class 377/2 four-car EMU No. 377 207 of Southern passes Headstone Lane at speed on a Watford Jct.–Brighton service, 25 June 2008.

Left: Seen south of Harrow and Wealdstone on a Watford Jct.–Brighton service is Southern express Class 377/2 four-car EMU No. 377 210, 2 July 2008.

Above left: Heading towards London Bridge at Sydenham is Class 377/1 four-car EMU No. 377 157 of Southern, 12 June 2009.

Above right: Speeding through Sydenham is Southern's express Class 377/4 four-car EMU No. 377 407 on a London Bridge–Brighton service, 12 June 2009.

Right: Class 377/5 four-car EMU No. 377 516 of First Capital Connect in their 'urban lights' livery passing East Hyde on a Brighton–Luton service, 15 April 2014.

Above left: Passing Thrales End, north of Wheathampstead, is First Capital Connect's Class 377/5 four-car EMU No. 377 501 on a Luton-bound service, 15 April 2014.

Above right: With the impressive train shed of London Bridge now gone, outer suburban Class 377/6 five-car EMU No. 377 611 of Southern awaits departure at the now rather low-key rebuilt station on its way to Horsham, 12 September 2015.

Left: Inner suburban Class 378/0 three-car EMU No. 378 003 (later No. 308 203) of London Overground leaves Kensington Olympia on a Willesden–Clapham Jct. service, 6 April 2010.

Above left: Slowing for its stop at Hoxton is London Overground's Class 378/1 four-car EMU No. 378 141 on a Dalston Jct.–New Cross Gate service, 6 June 2010.

Above right: Made up to five cars – with a large notice on the cab front to prove it – Class 378/2 No. 378 211 approaches Norwood Junction on a Highbury and Islington–West Croydon service, 12 September 2015.

Bombardier (Derby) 25 kV AC Overhead Stansted Express/Express Class 379 Electrostar Four-car EMUs

In 2010–11 thirty four-car 25 kV AC Class 379 sets were built by Bombardier, Derby, for National Express East Anglia's Stansted Express and Liverpool Street–Cambridge services. The Class 379s' two-class accommodation is to a very high standard and the units have large luggage racks because of the nature of their duties. In addition, they have some advanced electrical equipment which it is intended to fit to Bombardier's next generation of Class 345 Aventra EMUs for Crossrail. They are gangwayed throughout.

Bottom left: Greater Anglia Class 379 express four-car EMU No. 379 011 *Ely Cathedral* in GA's white livery climbs Bethnal Green Bank on a Liverpool Street–Stansted Airport service, 30 August 2012.

Bottom right: Under a brooding sky, Greater Anglia Class 379 four-car EMU No. 379 021 sweeps through Bethnal Green on a Liverpool Street–Cambridge service, 30 August 2012.

Bombardier (Derby) 25 kV AC Overhead/750 V DC 3rd Rail Express Class 387 Electrostar Four-car EMUs

Because of the long lead time before the Siemens Desiro City Class 700s could be delivered for Thameslink, it was decided to order yet another class of Electrostars as a stop-gap: twenty-nine four-car dual-voltage Class 387/1 sets being built at Derby by Bombardier in 2014–15 to replace Class 319s. After delivery of the Class 700s, the 387/1s will be transferred to newly electrified First Great Western services; FGW will also receive eight new 387/3s currently on order. In addition, twenty-seven Class 387/2s are being built in 2016 for Gatwick Express, replacing Class 442s. The Class 372s are gangwayed throughout.

Coming off the Crystal Palace line via the flyover is Class 387/1 four-car EMU No. 387 122 of Thameslink negotiating Norwood Junction on a Luton–Brighton service, 12 September 2015.

Third Generation EMUs – Designs under Privatisation: Alstom Pendolino 2001–12

Alstom (Washwood Heath and Savigliano) 25 kV AC Overhead West Coast Main Line High Speed Express Class 390 Pendolino Eight-, Nine- and Eleven-car EMUs

When Virgin won the West Coast franchise in 1997, they were committed to replacing the existing Class 86, 87 and 90 locomotive-hauled trains with high-speed EMUs to make the most of the planned 140 mph upgrade of the 25 kV AC West Coast main line. The train chosen was Fiat Ferroviaria's tilting Pendolino design. Unfortunately, dramatic cost escalation of the WCML upgrade saw its maximum speed scaled back to 125 mph, much to the chagrin of Virgin. The Pendolinos thus could never make the most of their potential; nonetheless, they have proved highly successful.

Initially, thirty-four eight-car sets and nineteen nine-car sets were assembled in 2001–04 by Alstom, Washwood Heath, the bodies and tilting mechanisms being supplied by Fiat Ferroviaria's Savigliano plant and the bogies by SIG of Switzerland. These units were the last trains to be built at Washwood Heath before closure. Rapidly increasing passenger numbers saw the eight-car sets strengthened to nine cars in 2004–05, all sets being classified 390/0. Then in 2009–12 extra cars were built at Savigliano to strengthen thirty-one sets to eleven-car Class 390/1s (leaving twenty-two sets remaining as 390/0s after one set had been destroyed in the Grayrigg accident). In addition, four brand new eleven-car sets were built.

Interestingly, the Class 390 sets have no dedicated restaurant or buffet cars, but instead have a small kitchen in one of the driving cars of each set to serve first-class passengers at their seats and a walk-in shop in one of the standard-class trailers. The EMUs are gangwayed within sets.

Above left: Euston-bound high-speed express Pendolino Class 390/0 nine-car EMU No. 390 007, *Virgin Lady*, glides past Headstone Lane, 25 June 2008.

Above right: Virgin West Coast Class 390/0 nine-car EMU No. 390 005 *City of Wolverhampton* at Watford Jct., 13 October 2009.

Right: Class 390/1 Pendolino eleven-car EMU No. 390 151, *Virgin Ambassador*, (with promotional branding for the International Festival for Business 2015) of Virgin West Coast nearing Warrington (Bank Quay) on a Glasgow (Central)–Euston service, 12 August 2015.

Third Generation EMUs – Designs under Privatisation: Siemens Desiro Family 2003 and Continuing

Siemens (Uerdingen-Krefeld, Wien and Praha Zlicin) 25 kV AC Overhead Outer Suburban/Express Class 350 Desiro Four-car EMU

The Class 350/1s were originally ordered for South West Trains as Class 450/2 DC five-car sets but the order was cancelled in this form. Instead, some sets were completed as four-car Class 450s for SWT, but bearing in mind experience gained with four Class 350 testbed sets (see Class 360 below), most of the Class 450/2 order was completed as dual-voltage DC/AC Class 350/1 four-car EMUs for a new joint Silverlink/Central Trains (later London Midland) regional express service on the West Coast main line's Euston–Birmingham and North West services, although in 2008–09 they were subleased to Southern until the new Class 377s arrived. Thirty Class 350/1s were built at Siemens' Uerdingen and Praha works in 2004–05 with low-density, two-class accommodation and gangways throughout.

The Class 350/1s proved successful from the outset and were followed by thirty-seven Class 350/2s, built at Uerdingen, Wien and Praha in 2008–09 for London Midland. These differed from the earlier sets by being single-voltage AC units with higher-density seating for outer suburban use and have replaced Class 321s on the WCML. Then came ten Class 350/3s built in 2014 at Uerdingen which were a single-voltage AC version of the 350/1s; they provided increased capacity on London Midland regional express services. Another ten AC Class 350/4s were built in 2013–14 at Uerdingen for Trans Pennine Express's Manchester Airport–Edinburgh/Glasgow service and completed with two-class, low-density, express accommodation.

Siemens (Uerdingen-Krefeld and Wien) 25 kV AC Overhead Outer Suburban/Express/Heathrow Connect Class 360 Desiro Four- and Five-car EMUs

The first Class 360s to be built by Siemens (at Uerdingen) in 2002 were the 360/2s – although they were not, in fact, completed as 360s but as Class 350 four-car testbeds. The four prototype sets were built with gangways throughout. In 2005 they were then rebuilt (with the central gangway in the cab removed and with all standard-class accommodation) as Class 360/2s specifically for Heathrow Connect services and an additional new unit constructed. In 2006–07 all

Above left: Arriving in Euston on a service from Northampton is London Midland Class 350/1 'Desiro' four-car outer suburban EMU No. 350 120, still in the unbranded grey and blue livery of the joint Silverlink/Central Trains service on the West Coast main line; January 2008.

Above right: Class 350/1 four-car EMU No. 350 118 of London Midland, but on hire to Southern, stops at Kensington Olympia on a Milton Keynes–East Croydon service, 18 September 2009.

Right: Seen passing Headstone Lane is London Midland Class 350/2 outer suburban four-car EMU No. 350 232 on a Euston–Milton Keynes service, 14 October 2009.

the sets were strengthened to five-car sets by the addition of new cars.

The twenty-one Class 360/0 four-car sets were built in 2002–03 by Siemens in their Uerdingen and Wien works for the 25 kV AC Great Eastern services and were the first UK order for the Desiro family. They are very similar to the rebuilt Class 360/2s but with first-class accommodation and with gangways throughout. They replaced Class 312 slam-door EMUs and Class 321 EMUs on Liverpool Street–Clacton/Walton-on-the-Naze/Colchester/Ipswich services.

Siemens (Uerdingen-Krefeld) 25 kV AC Overhead Outer Suburban Class 380 Desiro Three- and Four-car EMUs

Twenty-two three-car Class 380/1s were built by Siemens in Krefeld in 2009–10 and originally ordered by Transport Scotland for the now cancelled Glasgow Airport Rail Link; instead they are used on the Stratchclyde 25 kV AC system around Glasgow (replacing Class 318s and 334s), namely the Ayrshire coast and Inverclyde services. Later, they spread to other central Scotland services. In 2010–11 sixteen four-car Class 380/1s replaced Class 322s on the North Berwick line out of Edinburgh Waverley, but they are also used on Strathclyde services. The Class 380s have sloping cab-ends with gangways which is a feature new to Desiro designs. They have all standard-class accommodation. Surprisingly, the Class 380s had a protracted introduction because of teething troubles, even though the Desiro was a well-proven design.

Siemens (Wien and Uerdingen-Krefeld) 750 V DC 3rd Rail Express Class 444 Desiro (or 5-DES) Five-car EMUs

Siemens's Wien and Uerdingen works built forty-five Class 444s in 2003–04 to replace slam-door stock (4-CIGs and 4-BIGs) on South West Trains' express services out of Waterloo to Bournemouth/Weymouth and Portsmouth. They have low-density seating, are equipped with a miniature buffet and are gangwayed throughout. The Class 444 is sometimes described as the Rolls Royce of the Desiro fleet. They replaced 4-CEP/BEP/CIG/BIG and VEP slam-door stock and even the relatively modern Class 442 (5-WES) EMUs.

Siemens (Uerdingen-Krefeld and Wien) 25 kV AC Overhead Outer Suburban/Express Class 450 Desiro (or 4-DES) Four-car EMUs

The 127 Class 450 sets were built at Siemens's Uerdingen and Wien works in 2002–07 for South West Trains' outer suburban and main line semi-fast services out of Waterloo, replacing 4-VEP slam-door units. They are gangwayed throughout and have first- and standard-class accommodation but of a higher density than their sister Class 444s. The cab-ends are also slightly different.

Originally 117 four-car sets and thirty-two five-car sets (450/2) were ordered, but the 450/2s were cancelled because of the Strategic Rail Authority's refusal to lengthen the platforms necessary to cater for two 450/2s coupled together; instead, ten sets from this order were completed as four-car Class 450s but most were completed as dual-voltage Class 350/1s instead.

Above left: Two Class 360/0s Desiros outer suburban/express four-car EMUs of ONE, with No. 360 105 in the rear, are passing Pudding Mill Lane on a Liverpool Street–Clacton service, 3 October 2007. The set is still almost entirely in First Great Eastern indigo blue livery with 'swish' and Great Eastern branding, but with the First logos removed.

Above right: Approaching Hayes and Harlington is First Heathrow Connect Desiro Class 360/2 five-car EMU No. 360 203 on a Paddington–Heathrow Airport service, 7 April 2008.

Right: At its last stop before Liverpool Street, Greater Anglia outer suburban/express Class 360/0 four-car EMU No. 360 103 poses in the sun at Stratford, 30 August 2012. The set is in a hybrid livery consisting of a First Great Eastern blue base with the addition of a National Express East Anglia white stripe and an overlay of GA branding.

Above left: Scotrail outer suburban Desiro Class 380/0 three-car EMU No. 380 004 departs Paisley Gilmour Street on a Largs–Glasgow Central service.

Above right: Class 380/1 four-car EMU No. 380 109 of Scotrail departs Paisley Gilmour Street on an Ayr–Glasgow Central service.

Left: Class 444 (or 5-DES) five-car EMU No. 444 034 of South West Trains zooms through the art deco station of Surbiton on a Waterloo–Weymouth service, 24 March 2009. The set is in SWT's long distance/express red, white, blue, black and orange livery.

As built, the Class 450s were of one uniform configuration, but in 2008 twenty-eight sets were modified as Class 350/5HCs (the original sets becoming 350/0). These high-capacity units were used on inner suburban services; they had the first-class seating replaced with higher-density standard class seats and some of their standard class seats removed to create more standing room. However, with the reformation of the Juniper Class 358s, it was decided in 2013 to reinstate the first-class accommodation, although the units retained their 350/5 classification due to other differences in their seating arrangements.

Above: Seen nearing Surbiton is South West Trains Express Class 444 (or 5-DES) five-car EMU No. 444 012 on a Waterloo–Portsmouth service, 24 March 2009.

Right: Approaching Clapham Jct. is South West Trains outer suburban Class 450/0 (or 4-DES) four-car EMU No. 450 083 in SWT's outer suburban livery on a Waterloo–Basingstoke service, 20 July 2007.

Above left: Nearing Clapham Jct. is Waterloo-bound South West Trains Class 450/5HC (or 4-DES) four-car EMU No. 450 551, 7 April 2008.

Above right: Crossing Barnes Bridge on a Waterloo–Brentford–Waterloo circular service is South West Trains Class 450/0 (or 4-DES) four-car EMU No. 450 031 in SWT's outer suburban livery, 7 April 2008.

Left: South West Trains Class 450/5HC (or 4-DES) four-car EMU No. 450 570 in SWT's outer suburban livery at Barnes Bridge station on a Waterloo–Brentford–Waterloo service, 7 April 2008.

Third Generation EMUs – Designs under Privatisation: Hitachi Javelin 2006–09

Hitachi (Kasado) 25 kV AC Overhead/750 V DC 3rd Rail HS1 Domestic Class 395 Javelin Six-car EMUs

The six-car Class 395s were designed for high-speed (140 mph) outer suburban services on the 25 kV AC HS1 and beyond into Kent on conventional 750 V DC lines. Hitachi's Kasedo factory built twenty-nine sets in 2006–09. They were also used on the St. Pancras International–Stratford Olympic Javelin Shuttle service for the 2012 Olympics, the name Javelin sticking as a name for the class. All accommodation is standard class and gangwayed within sets only.

Just terminated at St Pancras is Southeastern High Speed Suburban Javelin six-car EMU No. 395 008 (later named *Ben Ainslea*), 2 February 2010.

Bibliography

Brown, David, *Southern Electric – A New History*, Vol:1 and Vol:2 (St Leonards on Sea, Capital Transport Publishing, 2010)

Butlin, Ashley Kenneth, *British Multiple Units Volume 1 Classes 302–390* (Craik, Coorlea Publishing, 2001)

Butlin, Ashley Kenneth, *British Multiple Units Volume 2 Classes 410–499 & 508* (Craik, Coorlea Publishing, 2004)

Cable, David, *Lost Liveries of Privatisation in Colour* (Hersham, Ian Allan Publishing, 2009)

Cable, David, *BR Passenger Sectors in Colour* (Hersham, Ian Allan Publishing, 2012)

Cadwallader, Jonathan and Martin Jenkins, *Merseyside Electrics* (Hersham, Ian Allan Publishing, 2012)

Emerson, Andrew, *Underground and Overground Trains* (St Leonards on Sea, Capital Transport Publishing, 2015)

Hendry, Robert, *British Railway Coaching Stock in Colour* (Hersham, Ian Allan Publishing, 2002)

Hendry, Robert, *British Railway Coaching Stock in Colour since 1960* (Hersham, Ian Allan Publishing, 2006)

Longworth, Hugh, *British Railways Electric Multiple Units to 1975* (Hersham, Ian Allan Publishing, 2015)

Marsden, Colin J., *The AC Electrics* (Oxford Publishing Co., 2007)

Marsden, Colin J., *The DC Electrics* (Oxford Publishing Co., 2008)

Marsden, Colin J., *Locomotives Illustrated No. 178 Desiro EMUs* (Hersham, Ian Allan Publishing, 2009)

Marsden, Colin J., *Locomotives Illustrated No. 183 First Generation Eastern Region (GE) Electric Multiple Units* (Hersham, Ian Allan Publishing, 2010)

Marsden, Colin J., *Locomotives Illustrated No. 194 The Electrostar Family – Classes 357, 375–379* (Hersham, Ian Allan Publishing, 2012)

Marsden, Colin J., *Locomotives Illustrated No. 214 Southern Design Electric Multiple Units* (Hersham, Ian Allan Publishing, 2014)

Marsden, Colin J., *Southern Electric Multiple-Units 1898–48* (Hersham, Ian Allan Publishing, 1983)

Marsden, Colin J., *Southern Electric Multiple-Units 1948–83* (Hersham, Ian Allan Publishing, 1983)

Marsden, Colin J., *DMU and EMU Recognition Guide* (Hersham, Ian Allan Publishing, 2013)

Moody, G.T., *Southern Electric 1909–79* (Hersham, Ian Allan Publishing, 1979)

Oliver, Bruce, *Southern Region Electrics in Colour* (Hersham, Ian Allan Publishing, 2008)

Oliver, Bruce, *Southern EMUs before Privatisation in Colour* (Hersham, Ian Allan Publishing, 2010)

Oliver, Bruce, *Southern EMUs since Privatisation in Colour* (Hersham, Ian Allan Publishing, 2011)

Pritchard, Robert and Peter Hall, *Electric Multiple Units* (Sheffield, Platform 5 Publishing, various years)

Abbreviations

AC   alternating current
BR   British Railways (1948–65), British Rail (1965–1994/97)
BREL   British Rail Engineering Ltd
DC   direct current
DMU   diesel multiple unit (mechanical or hydraulic transmission)
DEMU   diesel electric multiple unit (i.e. electric transmission)
ECML   East Coast Main Line
ECS   empty coaching stock
EMU   electric multiple unit (AC and/or DC supply)
ER   Eastern Region of BR
FCC   First Capital Connect
FGW   First Great Western
GA   Greater Anglia
GE   Great Eastern (lines of the ER)
GEML   Great Eastern Main Line
GN   Great Northern (lines of the ER)

LM   London Midland (service franchisee under privatisation)
LMR   London Midland Region of BR
LO   London Overground
LT&S   London Tilbury & Southend (lines of ER)
MU   multiple unit
NER   North Eastern Region of BR
NSE   Network South East of BR
NXEA   National Express East Anglia
PTE   Passenger Transport Executive
ScR   Scottish Region of BR
SR   Southern Region of BR
SWT   South West Trains
TfL   Transport for London
TOPS   Total Operations Processing System
TSO   Trailer Second Open or, from 11 May 1987, Trailer Standard Open
WCML   West Coast Main Line